# RENEWED EACH MORNING
## REFLECTIONS FROM THE ROCKING CHAIR

### PHILIP M. KANFUSH, O.S.B.

Saint Vincent Archabbey Publications
300 Fraser Purchase Road
Latrobe, Pennsylvania 15650-2690
http://www.stvincentstore.com/

**Library of Congress Cataloging-in-Publication Data**

Kanfush, Philip M., 1962 —

Renewed each morning : reflections from the rocking chair / Philip M. Kanfush.

p. cm.

ISBN 0-9708216-4-6

1. Meditations. 2. Catholic Church -- Prayer-books and devotations--English. I. Title.

BX2182.3.K36 2004

242--dc22          2004062339

CIP

**Printed in the United States of America**

Cover photo, Lancaster County, Pennsylvania by Colin Stebbins

Book design and editing, author photo,
by Kimberley A. Opatka-Metzgar

# ADDITIONAL PERMISSIONS

I very gratefully acknowledge those
whose assistance, encouragement and support
made this project possible:

Kimberley Opatka-Metzgar
Judith Regula
The parishioners of the Saint Vincent Basilica Parish,
Archabbot Douglas R. Nowicki, O.S.B.,
and
my brother monks at Saint Vincent Archabbey.

# CONTENTS

*Listen to me, you who pursue justice,*
*who seek the Lord;*
*Look to the rock from which you were hewn,*
*to the pit from which you were quarried;*
*Look to Abraham, your father,*
*and to Sarah, who gave you birth ... (Is 51:1-2)*

This book is lovingly dedicated to my parents,
Philip and Elizabeth (Farland) Kanfush,
who taught me,
by their steadfast faith and constant example
how to pray.

# FOREWORD
# REFLECTIONS FROM
# A ROCKING CHAIR?

When I first became an uncle, I learned the value of a good rocking chair. And long before I became a monk, my rocking chair became my sacred space, my place of prayer. My rocking chair is the sacred space where I reflect on God's word as it unfolds in my life, and pray. This heirloom rocking chair, the same one in which I found so much joy and peace rocking my first nephew, has gone everywhere that my adult life has taken me. It came with me to the monastery. It was in my college office where I advised my teacher education students and then later in my parish office. Now my precious rocking chair resides in my Life Skills Support classroom at the Clelian Heights School for Exceptional Children where I currently teach.

I originally wrote the brief essays contained in this book for my parishioners at the Saint Vincent Basilica Parish in Latrobe, Pennsylvania, which was my first assignment after I was ordained a priest. These reflections, which were printed in the parish's weekly bulletin, were one venue in which, as a part of the teaching office of the priesthood, I hoped to share with my parishioners the fruit of my "rocking chair" prayer times. That is the reason that they were originally titled *Reflections from the*

*Rocking Chair.*

However, the primary title for this collection, *Renewed Each Morning*, was derived from the Book of Lamentations:

> "*The favors of the* LORD *are not exhausted,*
>> *his mercies are not spent;*
> *They are renewed each morning,*
>> *so great is his faithfulness*" (3:22-23).

This single verse of scripture, perhaps more than any other, has held great personal meaning for me, and has come to undergird my entire belief system: Our loving Father never, ever, leaves us bereft of hope.

God constantly whispers his love for us in the depths of our hearts, but often the "noise" of daily life drowns out His song. We all need a sacred space where we can rest in stillness and allow the Lord to speak to our hearts. Maybe your sacred space is your kitchen table, your study, a favorite chair or even your porch. Perhaps your sacred space is best found outdoors. After all:

> "*the heavens declare the glory of God;*
>> *the sky proclaims its builder's craft*" (Ps 19:2).

My hope is that this collection of reflections will help you to find a space in your world where you can spend some moments each day with the Lord. Rest quietly in your sacred space. Maybe take a walk with Him. Breathe slowly and deeply, quiet your mind. Repeat a favorite Scripture verse. Let God speak to your heart. Even if it is just long enough for a cup of tea, you will find healing and peace.

*Father Philip, O.S.B.*

# 1
# CHOICES

*There is need of only one thing. Mary has chosen the better part and it will not be taken from her.* (Luke 10:42)

Dingle Shore, County Kerry, Ireland.  Photo by Melissa Lynch.

# CALL TO HOPE

When the Christmas season draws to its close with the Baptism of the Lord, our focus turns to the New Year. Many of us engage in the ancient custom of setting New Year's resolutions. These may take the form of making improvements in our lives. Some people may recommit themselves to working on their physical appearance, planning rigorous diets and exercise regimens. Others may feel impelled to make time for hobbies, reading or studies. For me, all of these have been resolutions through the years, and they can be counted upon to surface each year at this time like old friends. But before long, as the winter drags on, I find myself engaged in mortal combat with them — and with myself — my treasured friends transformed into bitter enemies.

Our resolutions, whatever form they might take, demonstrate our strong sense of hope — a hope for a future that we perceive to be better than our past or present — our hope for ourselves, that we can extend our possibilities.

It seems to me that it works much the same way with our spiritual lives. Many of us make renewed efforts to work on our relationship with God during the Advent season. We may avail ourselves of the sacrament of Reconciliation, pledging to make an effort in those areas of our lives that are lacking in virtue. But before long, we find ourselves falling into the same old bad habits. The situation is not unlike our struggle with our New Year's resolutions.

It takes constant vigilance. There are two metaphors that I find helpful to describe why we have to keep working on our spiritual lives. One was given to me by a priest when I was a junior monk. As one who likes to garden, it made great sense to me. He likened our bad habits to weeds in our garden. We have to keep on top of the situation, weeding regularly, or soon our gardens become overrun and lose their beauty.

The second metaphor came to me from a novel I once read called *Five for Sorrow, Ten for Joy* by Rumer Godden. The book tells the story of a group of nuns. Early in the novel, when their new chaplain arrives, he witnesses the sisters' daily chapter of faults, the custom by which the nuns come together each evening and publicly admit all the ways in which each has failed to live according to the Order's Rule during that day. The priest, shocked by this custom, questions the prioress about how the sisters could possibly have faults so serious that they warranted a daily public admission. But when he has been with them long enough to begin to understand the sisters as people, the new chaplain comes to recognize that the sisters, some of whom have converted after lives of crime, understand the insidious power of sin. Seemingly small sins can erode our spiritual lives in much the same way that, over time, water can wear away a mountain.

As can be the case with our New Year's resolutions, our spiritual intentions can often go off course. When this happens, we need to weed the garden and patch the sidewalk. We do this by bringing our struggle back to the sacrament of Reconciliation to be healed. We shouldn't wait until Christmas or Easter to do so.

And in just the same way, when we find ourselves drifting away from our New Year's resolutions, we shouldn't allow ourselves to become disgusted or depressed. We simply need to redirect our efforts and recommit ourselves. Missing the mark doesn't mean failing -- we are, after all, a people of hope. *"May the eyes of [your] hearts be enlightened, that you may know what is the hope that belongs to his call, what are the niches of glory in his inheritance among the holy ones."* (Eph 1:18).

Even though it may not be New Year's right now, take some moments to reflect on your resolutions, spiritual and temporal. Are you missing the mark in any way? If so, don't try to be a super-hero. We can't do it all at once. Take just one of the steps necessary to live as the person of hope God has called you to be.

# SPIRITUAL CHICKEN POX

One February, my little friend Alex had the chicken pox. It got me to thinking. The chicken pox visited me about the same time of year when I was in the fifth grade. It wasn't very pleasant and it lasted a looooong time. Like a bad guest, the chicken pox was uncomfortable and boring and miserable. It just had to be endured.

Sometimes life is like the chicken pox. You know this when you feel like you are just spinning your wheels and getting nowhere. You are trying just as hard as you can, and yet, all around you, people seem to keep putting hurdles or stumbling blocks in your path. The most aggravating thing is the fact that the harder we work, the less progress we seem to make and the more criticism we get for even trying.

I think it's cabin fever. We reach that point in the winter where Christmas has come and gone, the flu has been going around, and I wonder if we're not all just weary and worn. It's chicken pox time.

That weariness shows its ugly head in all sorts of ways. Do you find yourself flying off the handle over seemingly stupid situations? Do you find yourself getting tense and angry because someone else hasn't affirmed your efforts? Do you find yourself wanting to just shut yourself off from everyone and everything? Yep, it's chicken pox time. If it's any consolation, you're not in it alone. There are lots of us right now struggling with the same feelings – it's a regular epidemic.

So, how does one treat the spiritual chicken pox? First of all, we begin by recognizing that there are two modes by which we can approach others who frustrate or even hurt us. We can react; or we can respond. Reacting is easy; we don't even need to think about it. Somebody does or says something we don't like and BAMMO! There's our reaction. It can be a bit like a volcano erupting. Reacting does nothing to address the situation – it only makes things worse. On the other hand, we can respond. Responding is a rational act – it implies that we have deferred answering the situation. It means that we have chosen to step back and think before we say anything to the person who has offended us. It means we have chosen to distance ourselves from the offender long enough to allow God to guide us. Obviously, the Godly person makes a choice to respond rather than react.

When we are feeling this way, we have to be careful. The tendency is to react from our emotions – which can open a door to sin – rather than to make a carefully considered, faith-driven response. *"Be sober and alert. Your opponent the devil is prowling around like a roaring lion looking for [someone] to devour. Resist him, steadfast in faith"* (1Peter 5:8-9a).

Don't let the chicken pox get the best of you. Be on top of your game and choose to respond rather than react to those who get on your nerves. Pause for just a moment, and you can break the cycle of emotion and negativism. You can close the door to sin.

# A CHANGE IN ATTITUDE

Groundhog Day is an interesting tradition. According to Bill Anderson's *Groundhog Day 1886-1992,* the Groundhog Day Festival celebrated each year on February 2nd in Punxsutawney is rooted in ancient traditions. The Roman Legions brought the tradition to the Germans, who believed that the hedgehog, seeing its shadow, predicted six more weeks of winter. The German settlers, finding groundhogs in abundance, adopted them in place of the European hedgehog. Beginning in 1887, Punxsutawney Phil has consistently prophesied the arrival of spring, though not always as early a spring as we might like.

There has even been a movie produced about Groundhog Day. *Groundhog Day* is about a Pittsburgh weather man, played by Bill Murray, who goes to Punxsutawney to report on the Groundhog Festival, and who, through a twist of fate, is forced to relive Groundhog Day over 20 times. The movie is a comedy, but it also has a serious lesson to teach us.

Murray's character is compelled to live the same day over and over again because he doesn't learn from his mistakes. He repeats them again and again. Until he changes his attitude, he is doomed to repeat his mistakes.

The same is true of us. So often we find ourselves in destructive cycles of unhealthy choices. When we find ourselves caught in patterns of bad decision making we can begin to feel trapped. We repeat the same mistakes again and again, and it feels as though we're caught in a web from which we can never break free. Whether it comes down to our infidelity to our diets, our exercise regimens, our relationships or our faith, we all experience patterns that seem beyond our control — but they are not.

We do have control; we can change the choices we make — if we want to. It all begins with a change in attitude. In the movie *Groundhog Day*, Murray gradually stops repeating February 2nd when he changes his approach to life. And we can break the destructive patterns in our lives when we change our perspective. When we allow ourselves to rely on God's help, we can break the patterns that seem to enslave us.

*"I raise my eyes toward the mountains.*
*From where will my help come?*
*My help comes from the LORD,*
*the maker of heaven and earth."* (Ps 121:1-2).

*"I have the strength for everything through him who empowers me."* (Phil 4:13).

What area of your life makes you feel foolish or frustrated? Give it to God in prayer each day. Allow Christ's healing love to engulf you and set you free. You may not overcome an ingrained pattern of behavior in just one week, but do not lose hope! Have patience. The Lord will set you free.

# CHECK IT AT THE DOOR

When I was growing up I used to watch *Mister Rogers' Neighborhood* on television. Like most children, I was spellbound by his gentle voice and learned a great deal about caring and compassion from watching Mr. Rogers. As an adult, I look back on the show with a certain amount of nostalgia, but there was one thing about the show that stuck with me. It was a lesson that Mr. Rogers taught me very, very subtly, but one that has stayed with me nonetheless.

This lesson came from the beginning and end of each episode. Each day, as Mr. Rogers came into the set, he would take off his jacket, hang it up and put on a sweater. Then he would change from street shoes into tennis shoes. All this while Mr. Rogers sang that song that became woven into the fabric of my childhood, *Won't You Be My Neighbor?* At the end of the show, he repeated the process in reverse. As I look back, this simple set of actions has powerful meaning for me.

Each day, we juggle a multitude of problems, hurts and disappointments. Financial struggles, relationship problems, career difficulties can all seem insurmountable, and seem to overwhelm us. When we are having a bad morning at home, it often overflows into our workday, making that terrible. Or, when we have a rough day at work, we take the trouble home with us, where it spills out into our family life, where we find ourselves churlish and impatient with those we love.

The lesson about healthy adulthood that Mr. Rogers taught me is to shake off my home life problems, like he did his jacket and hard shoes, so that I can focus on my work in the morning, and, most importantly, to hang up the difficulties of my workday like he did his sweater or kick them away at the end of the day as he did his tennis shoes. Our families and friends do not know about the difficulties of our workday, and they probably could not have done anything to make the day any better, so there is no reason to trouble them with everything that has gone wrong in the course of day. Life is far too short to let our work troubles sour our home lives. Of course, it is good to talk with our families and friends about our worries and concerns, but too often, that kind of productive sharing gets drowned in the deluge of emotional baggage that we carry through the door with us.

Time with family and friends is meant to be treasured. It is a gift that we receive freely from the hand of God. We can choose not to allow the fever of our day to infect our home life. Consider this admonition of the ancients:

*Better a dry crust with peace*
*than a house full of feasting with strife* (Prov 17: 1).

The next time you find yourself having a bad day, hang up your troubles like Mr. Rogers' sweater before you go home.

# WINDS OF FORGIVENESS

One balmy, blustery morning in March, when my students at the Clelian Heights School for Exceptional Children were feeling particularly rambunctious, I decided to move my addition lesson outdoors, giving in to all of their fidgety energy. So I modified my lesson, grabbed the bucket of sidewalk chalk out of the cupboard, lined up my little troops and headed for the playground. There we drew number lines on the pavement, and then hopped our addition problems along the number lines rather than sitting indoors, working our sums with paper and pencil. Later in the day, when we were back outdoors for recess, I was surprised to see that their number lines had almost disappeared. I realized that the wind was erasing our work, and found myself recalling the gospel story of the woman caught in adultery.

In John's familiar account of the incident, the Pharisees brought a woman caught in adultery to Jesus while he was in the middle of teaching a crowd of people. It is not hard to imagine how the Pharisees were trying to cause a scene and to put Jesus on the spot in front of his followers. They said to him, *"Teacher, this woman was caught in the very act of commit-*

*ting adultery. Now in the law, Moses commanded us to stone such women. What do you say?" ...Jesus bent down and began to write on the ground with his finger. But when they continued asking him, he straightened up and said to them, "Let the one among you who is without sin be the first to throw a stone at her." Again he bent down and wrote on the ground. And in response they went away one by one ...* (John 8:4-9).

The reason that I was reminded of this story was because Jesus wrote on the ground, just like my students and I had. Nobody knows what Jesus wrote. John does not share that detail with us. There has been some speculation about the content of his writing among Scripture scholars. Some suggest Jesus may have been simply doodling, others that he was writing out the ten commandments and there are other theories as well. We will never know for sure. I like to think that he was writing out the woman's sin in the sand, so that the winds of forgiveness could erase it away, just like our number lines. I have no academic basis for it, but I do not believe that Jesus was writing out the ten commandments because those had been written in stone. Why? So that we might not forget them. When we consider that following those ten commandments leads us to do all manner of good acts, I think there is a powerful lesson for us.

A great many of us find it extremely difficult to let go of, much less forgive, an offense done to us. Yet how quickly we forget the good things people do for us. So often we jealously guard out hurts. I wonder about this tendency. There might be any number of reasons that we so readily forget the good deeds and many kindnesses shown us while we cling to the memory of even the slightest perceived insult to our pride. One theory that crossed my mind as a possible explanation for this tendency is that perhaps we hold on to hurts because they justify our own meanness and unkindness. We don't have to feel quite so guilty about treating someone uncharitably if we can trump up some prior charge against them to mitigate our own lack of love.

Unfortunately, the Christian vocation doesn't permit us this rationalization. *All bitterness, fury, anger, shouting, and reviling must be removed from you, along with all malice. [And] be kind to one another, compassionate, forgiving one another as God has forgiven you in Christ.* (Eph 4:31-32).

When someone has hurt us, maybe we should try actually writing the offense in a bowl of sand and then setting the bowl out in the yard where the wind can reach it. I wonder how quickly we might heal if we allowed ourselves to grieve over an injustice done us for just as long as the writing remains in the bowl of sand. It would be a hard lesson, but a very effective one.

Take a hard look around you. Have you been carving the wrong things in stone?????

# A NEW BEGINNING

Andrew Greeley tells the story of a Mom and Dad who *were packing up their things to go home from their summer vacation. They were very sad. They had to go home because the people who run schools make kids come back in August. The Mom and Dad were sad about the end of summer.*

*The family had enjoyed it enormously. Husband and wife, children and parents had been closer than they had been in a long time. The kids were getting older. There might never be another summer like this one. The parents, who were really not very old, felt kind of old, like life was slipping through their fingers. Why did summer have to end? Why did kids have to grow older?*

*Their eldest, a teenage boy, noticed his parents' strange mood and asked, "What's wrong with you two?" They explained their feelings to him. "Oh," he said wisely, "there's always next summer. It'll be different, but it will be better if we make it better."*

As I write this, school will be starting soon in most of our communities. Once again, we will see children at bus stops and the big yellow school buses that signal the start of another school year. It's hard to believe that summer is over already.

For some of us, going back to school presents two opposing

sets of feelings. On the one hand, we're excited about having new classes, new teachers and new possibilities. The beginning of the school year is a new beginning. On the other hand, whether we're going back to school ourselves or not, we hate to see summer draw to its close. It was wonderful having time to rest and relax.

Christian living is a lot like the start of a new school year. It's full of possibilities — but only if we're willing to let go of some things. Jesus tells us, *"whoever wishes to come after me must deny himself, take up his cross, and follow me"* (Matt: 16:24). The Christian life is a constant process of letting go, of dying little deaths – deaths to our own wishes and wills – to open up new possibilities. It means we have to let God lead us in the directions that He knows are good for us. We can't just stand still.

The teenage son in the story seems to have gained some Christian wisdom. Like his parents in the story, however, we often don't want to hear this message. Even so, we stand in good company. The apostles didn't want to hear Jesus' message about letting go either. They just wanted to let the good times keep rolling on. But growth requires change. And change necessarily involves letting go of the status quo to make room for something new. Growth inevitably involves little deaths. Our lives cannot be just an endless summer.

In a certain way, we are all called to go back to school. We are all called to be open to change and the new opportunities it presents to us. We are called to let go of whatever little attachments in our lives keep us from growing closer to God. We are called to accept the little deaths to getting our own way and having what we want all the time so that we will be ready when Jesus calls us to lay down our lives and step into His Kingdom forever.

Give some thought to what the start of a new school year symbolizes in your life. How well do you let go of the present so that you can grow into the future? If you find that some homework needs to be done in this area, ask Christ to give you the wisdom and the courage necessary to let go of your attachments and to grow in His love.

# IN FIRE GOLD IS TESTED

July is a joyful time in our monastery. Those who have completed their Novitiate profess their simple vows. Those who have completed their three years of simple vows profess their solemn vows, in which they are consecrated as monks for life. These two ceremonies are very moving and breathe life into the monastic community, but perhaps the most joyful event is the arrival of the new novices, men who come to us to begin their monastic journey and to test their vocation among us.

I remember my Novitiate year with great nostalgia. I arrived at the monastery just after 1 p.m. on July 1, 1993. It is our custom that the new novices arrive on July 1 to begin a 10-day pre-Novitiate retreat. On the tenth day, we were received into the Novitiate through a ceremony in which we were clothed with the monastic habit and received our tonsure. Tonsuring is an ancient tradition in which monks' hair was cut in a special way that made them stand out from other people. Today, the tonsure consists of five snips of hair taken from the crown of the novice's head and the sides, symbolic of the five wounds of Christ. He is then clothed in the tunic, belt and scapular of the Benedictine habit. The novice does not receive the cowl, or hood, that completes the habit until his first profession ceremony. This way, the novices stand out from the professed monks by a slight difference in their dress, but no one can tell the simply and solemnly professed monks apart, as both wear the full habit legislated by Saint Benedict in the *Holy Rule*. To me, there is a great comfort in knowing that I wear the same form of habit that Saint Benedict legislated for his monks almost 1500 years ago. Far from being outdated, it places me squarely in the stream of a powerful tradition and legacy.

During the Novitiate, the novice monk's life is strictly regulated. The primary purpose for these rules is to create an atmosphere of prayer and contemplation that is necessary if the novice is going to learn how to follow the *Holy Rule* of Saint Benedict properly. It must become a part of him, and that requires time and discipline. The monastic disciplines that the new novices are beginning to learn have to do with all that is central to the life of a monk. They have been learning how to serve at table in the monastery refectory, how to serve at altar and when and how to conduct themselves at the Community's common prayer at morning, midday and evening. They have learned how to come together for the night prayer, which the novices pray together, but which the rest of us are obligated to pray alone before we go to bed. They must learn to cultivate silence, and so are bound to keep "grand silence" after their night prayer and to learn to limit their speech in the hallways of the monastery, in the church and at other times and places. All of these disciplines become second nature to the monk and he automatically lives them as a result of this formation in the *Holy Rule*. But to the new novice, they present challenges and opportunities for personal growth. Coming from the mainstream of American life today, these disciplines are not easy to assimilate.

In all things, the novice is tested to see, as Saint Benedict puts it, *whether he truly seeks God, whether he shows eagerness for the work of God, for obedience and for trials* (RB 58:7). In Sirach we read:

> "My son, when you come to serve the LORD,
>> prepare yourself for trials.
> Be sincere of heart and steadfast,
>> undisturbed in time of adversity.
> Cling to him, forsake Him not;
>> thus will your future be great.
> Accept whatever befalls you,
>> in crushing misfortune be patient;
> For in fire gold is tested,
>> and worthy men in the crucible of humiliation.
> Trust God and he will help you;
>> make straight your ways and hope in him" (Sir 2:1-6).

I prayed this scripture a lot when I was a novice. I still do.

Take a few moments to reflect on the routines in your life. What distracting patterns can you eliminate? What new habits can you develop in your life to cultivate prayer and reflection on God's goodness?

# A GARMENT OF BRIGHTNESS

When a man comes to the monastery as a novice, he has a couple of senior monks assigned to work with him who are responsible for his formation as a monk. There is a Novice Master who trains the novices in the *Holy Rule* and a Socius (companion) who supervises the novices in the day to day activity of their first year of monastic life. I was fortunate when I was a novice to have a Socius who is a weaver. He learned the craft from his Novice Master. He did not teach me to weave during my novitiate, but I was able to assist him with setting up and threading his loom, and so I grew to appreciate the craft of weaving, its symmetry and form. Then, when I was a Junior monk, he taught me to weave. Since then I've spent many peaceful hours of solitude at my loom.

When a cloth is woven, the loom is threaded with lengthwise strands, often of a sturdier thread. This is called the warp. Then the weaver, works cross-wise threads or weft into the warp by hand. The process requires him to manipulate the warp threads using foot pedals on the loom. Meanwhile, the weaver works the weft shooting a shuttle holding the thread back and forth across the warp to create a pattern in the piece. It sounds complicated, but one develops a competency and the work becomes very rhythmic, freeing the mind for meditation.

Well, it seems to me that the art of weaving is an apt metaphor for human life. God strings the loom – he is responsible for providing the warp – and remember – the purpose of the warp is to provide the stability and durability for the tapestry or the cloth. We work the weft. We determine what scene will be depicted in the tapestry of our lives. But unlike the weaver who can go back and unravel the piece when he finds that he has made a mistake in the pattern, we can never completely undo our mistakes in life – we can compensate for the damage they cause, but they still leave a mark in our tapestry. So we have to be very careful about the choices we make. The warp is only so long, so we must weave carefully. As Job reminds us: *My days are swifter than a weaver's shuttle* (Job 7:6).

Reflect on your life. What choices have you made that have changed the direction of your life? What changes do you need to make now, so that the tapestry you present to God at the end of your life might be worthy of His gifts to you? An old Native American song, from *Songs of the Tewa*, suggests,

*Oh our Mother the Earth, oh our Father the Sky,*
*Your children are we, and with tired backs*
*We bring you the gifts that you love.*
*Then weave for us a garment of brightness;*
*May the warp be the white light of morning,*
*May the weft be the red light of eveing,*
*May the fringes be the falling rain,*
*May the border be the standing rainbow.*
*Thus weave for us a garment of brightness*
*That we may walk fittingly where birds sing,*
*That we may walk fittingly where grass is green,*
*Oh our Mother the Earth, oh our Father the Sky!*
Weave wisely, weave well.

# BACK TO CLASS

As I'm writing this, it's a Wednesday morning in mid-December. The parish office won't open for another two hours, but here I sit. Another semester is drawing to its close in the college. When I went to give my Organizational Behavior students their final exam yesterday, I found them all looking worn and bleary-eyed. Apparently they had been up late studying.

In what can only be considered divine justice, I sit here this morning, myself now worn and bleary-eyed. After their exam yesterday I quickly graded the tests and then sat down to read the students' journals. I figure I've read close to 450 pages since yesterday. The journals are actually quite interesting and reveal, far better than an exam ever could, just how much of what I taught them has been integrated into their lives. The reason I give the journal assignment is to force the students to use the class material to analyze situations in their lives. I find that if I make them apply the information or theories we've studied, they retain the knowledge far better.

Every week we return to the classroom, so to speak, in the celebration of the Liturgy of the Word at Mass. If we had to write a journal entry about something going on in our lives in light of what the lessons of the readings were, would we be able to apply them?

Last weekend I was away. A friend of mine from my college days got married. It was a treat for me to find a Catholic church in the next town to attend Mass on Saturday for the Holy Day of Obligation and on Sunday. As priests, we are almost always giving the homily and leading the liturgy. It was a treat to worship as an ordinary member of the congregation; to be taught instead of being the one to do the teaching.

We heard in the reading from Isaiah the promise that:

*"a shoot shall sprout from the stump of Jesse,*
*and from his roots a bud shall blossom.*
*The spirit of the LORD shall rest upon him:*
*a spirit of wisdom and of understanding,*
*A spirit of counsel and of strength*
*a spirit of knowledge and of fear of the LORD,*
*and his delight shall be the fear of the LORD."* (Is 11:1-3).

These are characteristics associated with the coming of the Messiah, and Isaiah assures us that their application will bring about a time of great peace, when *"the wolf shall be guest of a lamb"* (Is 11:6) and *"there shall be no harm or ruin on all my holy mountain"* (Is 11:9). A closer look at these characteristics reveals that these are, in fact, the very same gifts of the Holy Spirit that we received when we were confirmed: wisdom, understanding, counsel, fortitude, knowledge, reverence and piety. They are not to be kept on the shelf in our mental libraries. They are to be used. Isaiah tells us that *"the Gentiles shall seek out the root of Jesse, set up as a signal for the nations"* (11:10). We know that Christ and His cross are the signal, and it is amazing to recognize that this prophecy did come true: consider how many millions of souls have been drawn to Christ over the centuries.

Baptized into the mystical body of Christ, we take responsibility for continuing His mission. Now is the time to work to bring to the world that mission of peace. It is our responsibility. It is time to apply the lessons we have learned; to use the gifts with which we were sealed in our Confirmation. Reflect on your life. What is going on that requires you to use these gifts? Apply them. All around us are souls who have lost their way in some aspect of life or another. Sharing in the mystical life of Christ, we, too, are set up as a signal for the nations. We can choose to be a lighthouse for others to help them find their way. It doesn't require heroic virtue. Just use your gifts in your everyday life.

# GATHERING GRAIN

When I teach in the Education Department at Saint Vincent College, I often close my courses with the parable of the weeds and wheat. I read the parable to the students – typically right before we begin the final exam – partly to calm them down before the test, but mainly because the lesson in this parable is the most important thing I can teach my students about working with children.

In what seems to be conventional wisdom, the farmer tells his workers not to pull out the weeds because the wheat might be damaged. So he lets them grow together until harvest time, when they are separated, the wheat gathered into the barn and the weeds bundled for burning.

The original purpose of this parable in Matthew's gospel was to reassure the early Church. It had begun to be apparent, even as early as Matthew's time, that not everyone who made the profession of faith at baptism would live out his faith commitment perfectly. Some would fall away from the faith. And so Matthew recalled this teaching of Jesus and used it to give the Church hope. Everything will work out in the end.

What was true for the Church in Matthew's day is certainly

still true in our day — there are still good and bad Christians. But there's more to it than simply that. When I use the parable of the weeds and the wheat in my classroom, I try to impress upon my students, future teachers, that the most important impact we as teachers have on our students comes not through what content we teach them — in the end that's not the most important lesson. The most important impact we have on our students' lives is through how we treated them — whether we listened to the things they said to us; whether we took the time to care about their feelings and their world; whether we loved them, even if we didn't like them. You see, I point out to my students, you'll never really know the impact that you have on your students' lives. You won't see it, because they move on. You only have your students on loan. When you have them in your classroom, some students will seem like weeds; others will seem like wheat. Do not judge — do not write off the kids that you don't think will ever amount to much — because they just might. The most important thing to remember is that they are, after all, God's project, and God can change weeds into wheat. If you treat them with love and respect, they might just amount to something great — but you'll never know — except in the relatively few instances when they come back as adults to see you, or you read about them in the newspapers.

The same is true for each of us and our relationships with others. We will never know the impact — good or bad — that we've had on those who pass through our daily lives. I think that this parable should be applied by each and every one of us to areas in our own lives. That's certainly what Matthew intended by including it in his gospel. As God has been patient with us, so we must be patient with others. And that's really hard to do. It

means we must stop passing judgment on others based on ap-
pearances and first impressions. It also means treating everyone
fairly, whether we like them or not. It means being as kind to
those we can't stand as we are to those we love. It means toler-
ating weaknesses in others, because God has first tolerated our
weaknesses.

Take a minute to read the parable of the weeds and the
wheat. You'll find it in Matthew, chapter 13, verses 24-30. Reflect
on your life. In what ways has God been patient with you in your
failings? How does that teach you to treat others?

# THE PRINCE AND THE PAUPER

One of the benefits of attending an urban university is that you can walk just about anywhere you need to go. In the city, you encounter all sorts of interesting people when you are on foot. When I was a junior at the University of Pittsburgh, I dated a young woman who lived on the other side of campus from my fraternity house. One January evening, I was walking to her apartment to pick her up for our Saturday night date. It was a bitter cold night with a single digit wind chill. I was freezing even in my down ski jacket and gloves.

About half way to my girlfriend's apartment, I had just crossed where a side street intersected Fifth Avenue. I looked up as I passed a garbage can on the street corner in front of the Mellon Bank. Stooped there across the garbage can from me was a homeless man. I gauged him to be in his late twenties, not even a decade older than me. The man could have been my brother. We were close enough in age. He was just a little taller than I and had straggly brown hair hanging from under his filthy orange stocking cap. The man's green army coat was torn, tattered and stained from what must have been countless nights on the street. He had no gloves. His hands were dirty and chaffed from the cold. A study in contrasts, I stood there dressed for a night on the town in all my preppy finery. As he caught my gaze, he was holding a half-eaten lollipop in his hand that some passerby had tossed into the garbage can. He appeared to be considering whether he could pluck the debris that had gathered on it in order to salvage the candy. As I recall that evening, I realize that there was a crowd of about ten people waiting for the bus. None of them seemed to notice the homeless man at all. It was as if he were invisible.

As I passed, our eyes locked, and time seemed to stand still. His brown eyes challenged me in a look of defiance as we stood there sizing each other up, the prince and the pauper. In my youthful naiveté and arrogance, I recall thinking that he was disgusting. The moment ended and I continued on my way, never really pausing at all.

It never occurred to me that I might have been able to help him. It never occurred to me that I might have smiled at him or even said hello. It never occurred to me that I might have offered the man my gloves — I could easily have replaced them. It never occurred to me that I might have taken him into the Burger King next to the bank to buy him a cup of hot coffee and a warm sandwich. My girlfriend would have waited the few moments that would have taken. It never occurred to me that I might have looked on him with compassion instead of disgust. It never occurred to me until later that I might have been gazing into the eyes of Christ.

We each come into contact with an enormous number of people every day. Whether we speak to them or not, we communicate a message. Is that message one of love, of compassion, of acceptance, of judgment or ridicule? *He who mocks the poor blasphemes his Maker* (Prov 17:5). Think about the messages you are communicating to the world. Do they speak acceptance or apathy?

# 2
# HOMECOMING

*... Go home to your family and announce to them all that the Lord in his pity has done for you. (Mk. 5:19)*

Amish Country, Blair County, Pennsylvania. Photo by Kim Metzgar.

# STAND FIRM IN YOUR FAITH

I sometimes find myself wondering what it is about being young today that so many children are so troubled in heart and spirit. It seems to me that if we look at the TV listings in the newspaper, we can get some clues. I fear that American culture has made entertainment out of what used to be unspeakable. And I just don't get it. We have TV shows featuring all manner of crime: *America's Most Wanted, Cops, Crime Stories, Homicide: Life.* Then there are the talk shows. We can be thrilled as real life dramas unfold on talk shows like *Jerry Springer* and *Ricki Lake,* among others. The topics to which we are exposed on these shows can only be described as sordid. One *Inside Edition* show was all about provocative dances. Then there are the comedies. One evening I was treated to a few moments of *The Geena Davis Show,* whom I discovered, during prime time no less, lives with her fiancé, teaching all of America that cohabitation is acceptable. I saw in the newspaper the listing for *The Drew Carey Show* promoting an episode of which was titled, "Buzzie Wuzzie Liked His Beer." An episode of *That 70s Show* featured "Holy Crap: The Formans Skip Church" as the episode title. Is it just me, or does anyone else out there see a problem???? I only looked at the TV listings! What about movies, popular magazines, music lyrics, billboards and advertising media?

In the publication, *God's Little Devotional Book*, the story is told of a man who refused to conform to the prevailing culture. *As legend has it, a just and good man went to Sodom one day, hoping to save the city from God's judgment. He tried talking to first one individual and then the next, but nobody would engage in conversation with him. Next, he tried carrying a picket sign that had "Repent" written on it in large letters. Nobody paid any attention to his sign after an initial glance. Finally he began going from street to street and from marketplace to marketplace, shouting loudly, "Men and women, repent! What you are doing is wrong. It will kill you! It will destroy you!"*

*The people laughed at him, but still he went about shouting. One day, a person stopped him and said, "Stranger, can't you see that your shouting is useless?" The man replied, "Yes, I see that." The person then asked, "So why do you continue?"*

*The man said, "When I arrived in this city, I was convinced that I could change them. Now I continue shouting because I don't want them to change me."*

Considering that our children are being inundated with all manner of media which is completely antithetical to Christian values, perhaps we don't have to look too far to understand why child violence happens. Our children have been desensitized to Christian moral values. It may be that like the man in the legend, our cry of outrage at this situation will be unsuccessful at changing the kinds of TV viewing we are offered. But as we continue to be exposed to these media, we can become desensitized too. Maybe like the man in the legend, we need to cry out, if only to keep our moral judgment from being slowly eroded. *If you do not stand firm in your faith, you will not stand at all* (Is 7:9, [NIV]). This week, check out what your children, grandchildren, nieces or nephews are watching on TV. What do you find yourself watching? Perhaps now is the time to start encouraging reading a good book for entertainment.

# TATTERED TAPESTRY

So often I hear from people that they see no point or need in availing themselves of the Sacrament of Reconciliation. "I don't need to tell my sins to a priest," I'm told, "because I can confess them directly to God. I don't need a middle man." I'm sad to say it, but all that their opinion shows me is a self-centered view that betrays a misunderstanding of our interconnectedness. As members of the Church, we are incorporated through baptism into the Mystical Body of Christ. This means that everything I do affects every other member of that Body, and everything you do affects me. There is no such thing as private sin. Each person's sin touches all of us, like ripples in a pond. *For as in one body we have many parts, and all the parts do not have the same function, so we, though many, are one body in Christ and individually parts of one another* (Rom 12:4-5).

I like to use the analogy of a tapestry for the Mystical Body of Christ. Each of us represents a single thread, and the picture the tapestry presents is exceedingly beautiful. When I sin, if it's a venial sin, it creates a snag. It doesn't ruin the tapestry, but it does diminish its beauty. A mortal sin is like a tear in the tapestry. It *does* damage the picture — it creates a hole in the fabric. It ruins the tapestry for everyone. One of the reasons that it is necessary to confess our sins to a priest in the Sacrament of Reconciliation is the interconnectedness of all the members of the Mystical Body of Christ. The priest stands, not just as the representative of Christ, though he surely is that, but also as the representative of the Christian community whom we have wounded by our sin. That's why Reconciliation is so important. Even our most personal sins have communal implications.

A friend of mine who travels a lot on business once brought me back a greeting card from England. It is a beautiful card, done in ornate script reminiscent of medieval manuscript illustration. When I read the prayer on the card, I realized that my friend really understood me — understood my concerns about the man I believe that I'm called to be versus the man I'm afraid of becoming. I tried to find who wrote the prayer, but the best research tools at my disposal merely disclosed that the prayer is ascribed to an anonymous nun of the seventeenth century, presumably in England. As I read it, I find that the woman who wrote the prayer understood the true nature of sin. She also understood herself. It's a good prayer for all of us. Reflect on the nun's prayer and come to the Sacrament of Reconciliation.

*17th Century Nun's Prayer*

*Lord, Thou knowest better than I know myself, that I am growing older and will someday be old. Keep me from the fatal habit of thinking I must say something on every subject and on every occasion. Release me from craving to straighten out everybody's affairs. Make me thoughtful but not moody; helpful but not bossy. With my vast store of wisdom, it seems a pity not to use it all, but Thou knowest Lord that I want a few friends at the end.*

*Keep my mind free from the recital of endless details; give me wings to get to the point. Seal my lips on my aches and pains. They are increasing, and love of rehearsing them is becoming sweeter as* the years go by. I dare not ask for grace enough to enjoy the tales of others' pains, but help me to endure them with patience.

I dare not ask for improved memory, but for a growing humility and a lessing cocksureness when my memory seems to clash with the memories of others. Teach me the glorious lesson that occasionally I may be mistaken.

Keep me reasonably sweet; I do not want to be a Saint — some of them are so hard to live with — but a sour old person is one of the crowning works of the devil. Give me the ability to see good things in unexpected places, and talents in unexpected people. And, give me, O Lord, the grace to tell them so. AMEN

# SEALED BY HIS HAND

When harvest time has passed and we have celebrated the feasts of All Saints and All Souls, I find myself with an unusual feeling of stillness. In the world of Nature, I notice a chill in the air and a calm — the frenetic gathering time has ended and there is less activity to be observed among the wildlife. In the world of secular concerns also, there is a lull. Halloween has come and gone, the costumes have been folded away for another year, and finally the avalanche of election propaganda has subsided. We have a week or two of quiet before Thanksgiving arrives and the frantic rush of Christmas — the shopping, the baking and the parties — begins.

This brief respite should not be wasted. In my own Maronite Catholic tradition, our new liturgical year begins with what we call "The Sunday of the Consecration of the Church." It is an apt introduction to the liturgical year because it teaches us that the entire salvific mission of Christ in the world today takes place through His Church.

In both the Old and New Testaments, the term "corban" is used to refer to something consecrated to the Lord. An object was anointed with oil and then considered to be holy or set apart for the Lord. In the Old Testament, we read that priests, kings, the meeting tent and its utensils and even the Ark of the Covenant were anointed, and thus consecrated to the Lord. In the New Testament, Jesus himself is called the Messiah, the Christ, the Anointed One. The Church today continues the practice of anointing — catechumens, confirmandi, the sick, priests and bishops, church buildings and sacred vessels are all anointed to set apart these people, places and things for the Lord's service. This list includes all of us, since we were all anointed at our baptisms: *But the one who gives no security with you in Christ and who anointed us is God; he has also put his seal upon us and given the Spirit in our hearts as a first installment.* (2Cor1:21-22).

Enjoy some "down" time. Spend some of that time reflecting on your personal relationship with the Christ. How well are you living out your consecration to the Lord?

# A SEASON FOR HOPE

I have long marveled at the incredible wisdom of the early Church Fathers in setting the liturgical seasons. When the natural world is cold and damp, when death and darkness seem to reign, they give us the season of Advent to prepare us for the birth of the Messiah — to fill us with hope. It is my favorite of the liturgical seasons, steeped in prophecy and promise. Consider the timing of the feasts. In June, when the days were at their longest, we celebrated the birth of John the Baptist, who was sent to prepare the way of the Lord. He is the Forerunner, who said of Jesus, *He must increase; I must decrease* (Jn 3:30). Shortly after John's feast, the days do begin to grow shorter. They continue to decrease, until, when we have reached the shortest day of the year, we celebrate the birth of the Light of the World, Jesus. Then, daylight gradually starts to grow longer. The early Fathers used the natural rhythms of light and darkness to help us to appreciate the mystery of salvation history. I find their insight fascinating!

In the Western Church, where Advent allows us to enjoy up to four weeks of preparation, the readings at Mass recall the prophecies and promise of fulfillment. How beautiful our

Western tradition is! But in the Eastern churches, the custom varies. The Byzantine Church begins preparation for the Nativity of the Lord as early as November 15, with the Philip Fast. From then on the prayers of this venerable tradition repeatedly call us to prepare for the the coming of the Messiah, until on the Sunday before Christmas, special acknowledgement is paid to those who throughout the ages were heralds of Christ: *Lift up your voice, Zion, holy city of God; proclaim the blessed memory of the Fathers. With Abraham, Isaac and Jacob, we praise them with our songs. Behold how, with Judah and Levi, we glorify Moses, and Aaron, inspired of God. We celebrate with David, Joshua, Samuel. Let our songs preview the divine birth of Christ . . . Come Elisha, you who one day saw Elijah drawn off in a heavenly chariot of fire, together with Hezekiah and Josiah, rejoice! You inspired prophets, lead the dance for the Nativity of the Lord.*

In my own Maronite Rite, this preparation is also spread out over six weeks, each Sunday recalling the announcements to the principal witnesses of the Messiah's birth: first the Announcement to Zechariah, then the Annunciation to Mary, the Visitation to Elizabeth, the Birth of John the Baptist and the Revelation to Joseph. Finally, on the last Sunday before Christmas comes Genealogy Sunday, when the long list of Jesus' ancestors is read to call us to trust in God's plan of salvation already at work from the time of Adam's fall.

All of these varied traditions show the richness of the universal Church and challenge us to reflect on God's saving action throughout history — action which continues even to our day. Therein lies the great mystery of Advent: it at once celebrates what has already taken place in the fullness of time, as well as looks forward to Jesus' second coming, for which we must all prepare.

Get out your Bible. Look up some daily readings. Take a few minutes to reflect on them. Be amazed at how the prophets foretold the coming of the Messiah. What message of hope do they bring to your situation? Are there ways that you can decrease so that Christ's presence in your life can increase?

# OF FASTS AND FEASTS

One weekend I went to see the high school's production of Meredith Willson's musical, *The Music Man*. It is one of my favorite musicals because I grew up on the songs from *The Music Man*. The show was one of my father's favorites, and we'd see the movie at least annually. I would imagine that my sisters and I know the words to every song by heart; we heard them so many times when we were growing up. I can remember my mother singing them and us singing them with her.

My favorite part is near the end, when the whole town is chasing Professor Harold Hill to capture him for tar and feathering, and little Winthrop comes upon the Professor engaged in earnest conversation with his sister, Marian. Winthrop challenges the Professor for conning the people of River City all summer. He turns to Marian and asks her if she believed the Professor. She says that she did, even though she had discovered that he was a con man before he'd been in town three days. She tells her brother, *"I believe everything he ever said ... I know what he promised us and it all happened just like he said — the lights, the colors, the cymbals, the flags."* When Winthrop asks her when all these things happened, Marian responds, *"In the way every kid in this town walked around all summer and looked and acted, especially*

54

*you, and the parents too."*

Maybe we, like the good townspeople of River City, Iowa, in Willson's musical, need to pick up our heads and take pride in our communities and in our young people. Perhaps it's time we show them how proud we are of them. Even though what the Professor did in the musical was patently wrong, the story's happy ending reminds us that God can take the bad things that happen to us and make us grow in good ways in spite of them, if only we remain open to His Spirit working in our lives. It reminds us that God can work little miracles in our lives too. We need only cooperate with his grace.

I wonder if perhaps one reason why our young people find themselves caught up in problems with drugs, alcohol and violence is because they lack a sense of hope. Perhaps this has been our unfortunate legacy to them. One of the most important lessons I learned in my graduate studies in Special Education was the importance of using what are called positive behavioral supports. The implication of this approach in working with children is that instead of using punishment and scolding to correct inappropriate behaviors, we should design positive outcomes for them. Far from granting the children immunity from the consequences of their actions, this approach teaches them to take responsibility for the choices they make. If we structure opportunities for children to experience success in taking such responsibility, we also create opportunities to affirm them at every turn. The children grow in self-respect and develop positive self-concepts. They begin to feel competent and hopeful.

I wonder what our lives would be like if we used this approach, not only with our children, but with everyone in our lives. If instead of giving in to our natural inclination to judge, we made the choice to affirm others whenever we can. If instead of choosing to see the glass half empty, we chose to look at it as half full. Perhaps if we lived like this, we'd find our community built up and our children happy. Maybe our streets would be like those of River City in Willson's musical. We'd live in the freedom promised to God's children.

# POWERFULLY PIERCED

Sometimes, in my ministry to the sick, I am called upon to help the people I serve to prepare for death. I consider it a great privilege to serve in such an intimate capacity, because I believe, as my Novice Master once taught me, that the Holy Spirit is always very present to us in the "threshold moments" of life, those times when we are making decisions that will change the direction of our paths to the Kingdom and impact the paths of others. I have come to see how very present the Spirit is to those who find themselves standing on the biggest threshold – the one between life as we know it now and everlasting life. These are the times when their hearts and the hearts of those who love them are pierced by a sword.

In March, 1996, my sister Michaleen gave birth to her long-awaited second child, a daughter whom she and her husband, Scott, aptly named Hanna, a name that means, 'grace.' Within the first twenty-four hours after Hanna's birth, we learned that she had been born with a chromosomal anomaly. We were in-formed that Hanna might live for a few hours, a few days, a few weeks, or at most, a few months.

We were very greatly blessed; Hanna lived for exactly two

months to the day of her birth. We made the most of every one of those days, celebrating the gift of her life to the fullest. On the evening before Hanna died, I was preparing to return to the Archabbey after a visit with my sister, brother-in-law and Hanna at my parents' home. It was a beautiful spring evening and my sister followed me out to the car. I could tell that something was on Michaleen's mind, so I turned, leaning on the trunk of the car to face her.

This memory is frozen in my mind as if it had occurred yesterday. As she stood facing me, the setting sun framed her face. I said, "How are you doing Mike?" as I rubbed her forearms. She said to me, "Phil, every night I pray to Mary. I say, 'Mary, you had the strength to watch your Son die; help me to watch my baby die.'"

I don't recall what I said to that, or what my sister said next. I don't remember getting in my car and driving the hour and a half back to the Archabbey. I remember only the two of us frozen in time with the sun setting behind her in my arms and the words that she spoke. It was in that moment that I understood the healing power of God's grace. My sister's words were a sword that pierced my all too wounded heart.

All of the members of my family, devastated by the trauma of finally having a child only to learn that we must let her go all too soon, struggled with the mystery of Hanna's disability. I foolishly felt that my job, as the religious professional, was to find the answers for how this could happen to us. But there are no satisfactory answers. I wanted so desperately to be able to comfort these people whom I love so dearly, but I was empty. Like a dried corn husk in a chilling November wind, I had no answers, just very bitter and dark questions that I was far too fearful to voice, even in my private prayer. I find it ironic that while I was attempting to minister to my sister, she, the wounded mother, herself pierced by a sword, should instead minister to me in my brokenness. But, once again, such is God's mercy, where you least expect to find it.

In that graced threshold moment, the image that came to my mind with stunning clarity was that of Simeon and Anna, coming upon Mary and Joseph with the child Jesus in the Temple. As Luke tells it, Simeon blessed them and said to Mary his mother: *"This child is destined to be the downfall and the rise of many in Israel, a sign that will be opposed – and you yourself shall be pierced with a sword – so that the thoughts of many hearts may be laid bare."* (Luke 2:32-35)

What I understand now is that God does not pierce our hearts. He does not cause bad things to happen to us or to those we love, but He does make the most of the opportunity that our pierced hearts present to Him. I have learned that when life causes our hearts to be broken, when "the slings and arrows of outrageous fortune," as Shakespeare described it, tear into the very core of our being, when we have been pierced by swords, God makes use of the opening that the wound tears in our hardened hearts to pour in his healing grace.

This is a great mystery. The mechanics of how this grace operates in our hearts is beyond us. Every parent, every aunt or uncle, every person who has loved a child with disabilities can attest that the sword never goes away. The pain is omnipresent on some level, but I have come to understand that God's grace is also omnipresent, and where we learn to remain open to the Spirit working in and through our lives, that grace is a source of great healing and holiness. My sister's words to me on that memorable day literally saved me. It was her own openness to the Spirit of God working in her life that made her words life-giving for me and changed the direction my life, leading me to a ministry in special education. Each of us who has been wounded in this life has also been called to be life-giving in much the same way. We can choose to hoard our swords like squirrels frantically preparing for the cold, dark winter, licking our wounds and keeping them raw, or we can choose to be open to the power of grace in our lives and become a source of healing and growth for others, even as we find healing ourselves. The power of grace is always offered, but we must consciously choose our response. Choose wisely.

# RETURN TO ME

I remember when I was a kid thinking that Lent was all about "give ups." I'd usually give up cookies and candy — a grave sacrifice to a kid with a sweet tooth. Lent became an endurance test for me, a struggle to see if I could last until Easter. As I got older, the same concept applied, I just substituted desserts for cookies and candy.

In the past, we have overemphasized the penitential aspect of Lent. However, in the *Constitution on the Sacred Liturgy*, the Fathers of the Second Vatican Council remind us that Lent is marked by two themes, the baptismal and the penitential (CSL 109). We tend to forget, except at the Mass where we have the presence of the RCIA Candidates and Catechumens to remind us, that Lent has any relationship to baptism whatsoever.

Lent is a time when we can take stock of our relationship with the Lord and do the spiritual housecleaning that is necessary to prepare ourselves for the Triduum and the celebration of the great feast of Easter when we will renew our baptismal promises. This is not just a task for the RCIA. This time is important for all of us — and it goes way beyond giving up desserts!

The central theme of Lent is one of conversion — renewing our commitment to living our faith. This notion of conversion encompasses both the baptismal and the penitential themes of

Lent. *Even now, says the LORD, return to me with your whole heart* (Joel 2:12). While our conversion has been expressed in terms of fasting and making sacrifices – the "give ups" of our childhood, the kind of conversion to which God calls us during Lent is much more fundamental. Making sacrifices is important and can do us physical as well as spiritual good. But too often, we allow the "give up" to become the purpose of our whole Lenten observance, instead of the means to a greater spiritual end. *Rend your hearts, not your garments* (Joel 2:13) the Lord calls out to us. Mere external observance, if it is not a sign of a true inner conversion, is pointless.

> *This, rather is the fasting that I wish:*
> > *releasing those bound unjustly,*
> > *untying the thongs of the yoke;*
> *Setting free the oppressed,*
> > *breaking every yoke;*
> *Sharing your bread with the hungry,*
> > *sheltering the oppressed and the homeless;*
> *Clothing the naked when you see them,*
> > *and not turning your back on your own* (Is 58:6-7).

All these good works begin with prayer. Make working on your prayer life — spending more time with the Lord — your objective. As little as ten minutes each day could make a profound difference in your life. Take some time to reflect on what you can do to help you to review and renew your baptismal commitment. Choose a book to read, attend a community meal or learn something new about prayer. Do something, anything at all, to make your relationship with the Lord a greater part of your life.

> *Return to me, and I will return to you,*
> > *says the LORD* (Mal 3:7).

# PAY UP!!

There is a segment from Matthew's gospel in which the Pharisees try to trick Jesus into speaking against the Roman tax. Jesus, far from falling into their trap, asks them to show him a coin. He asks whose inscription appears on the coin, and then speaks the words that have become so familiar to us: *then repay to Caesar what belongs to Caesar and to God what belongs to God* (Mt 22:21).

There is a famous verse from Deuteronomy (6:4), the Shema, in which Moses enjoins on the people of Israel God's firm commandment, *Hear, O Israel! The LORD is our God, the LORD alone! Therefore, you shall love the LORD, your God, with all your heart, and with all your soul, and with all your strength.* Every Jew, from the days of Moses to Jesus' time and even to the present can quote this verse by heart. And so should every Christian be able because Jesus refers to it as the first and greatest commandment, and tells us that *the second is like it: You shall love your neighbor as yourself* (Mt 22:39).

I would be willing to assert that we do a very good job of "repaying to Caesar what belongs to Caesar." After all, most of us have no difficulty whatsoever living in the popular, secular culture with its values of individualism and getting ahead. This is how society measures success.

The question is, how well do we do repaying to God what belongs to God? We do this primarily by living out the Shema. That requires that Jesus be the Lord of our lives and that we love Him with our very being. Such love, when it is the driving force behind our lives, naturally flows out in love of neighbor.

Traditionally, the Church has operationalized this love in the Corporal and Spiritual Works of Mercy. The Corporal Works of Mercy are: to feed the hungry; to give drink to the thirsty; to clothe the naked; to give shelter to the homeless; to visit the sick; to visit the prisoner; and to bury the dead. The Spiritual Works of Mercy are: to instruct the ignorant; to counsel the doubtful; to admonish sinners; to bear wrongs patiently; to forgive offenses willingly; to comfort the afflicted and to pray for the living and the dead.

These make a wonderful examination of conscience or a checklist for how we're doing in repaying to God what belongs to God. Unfortunately, for many of us, an honest look at the Works of Mercy might not show us in too favorable a light. When is the last time, for example, that you admonished a sinner, instructed the ignorant in the ways of Christ or forgave offenses willingly? These actions are not what society teaches us that successful people do. Yet they are precisely what we are absolutely obliged to do by our baptism. These are the very ways that we show that we do, in fact, love the Lord our God with all our heart, all our soul and all our might. These are the ways we love our neighbor as ourselves.

If an honest and hard look at our lives shows us to be somewhat lacking in performing the Works of Mercy, we can always make a change. Pick just one of the Works of Mercy and make a concerted effort to perform it consistently. It will require discipline, but that is how we grow in the spiritual life. By making a few simple choices when opportunities present themselves, we grow in holiness. Take a chance and grow.

# BECAUSE SHE LOVED MUCH

In July we celebrate the feast day of Saint Mary Magdalene. From the time I was a small boy, she was one of my favorite saints. I couldn't have told you why back then, except that I liked her picture in the church. In our home church in Aliquippa, Saint Titus, there was a mosaic of Mary Magdalene kneeling at Golgotha with her arms around the base of the cross and Jesus' feet. Her face in the mosaic as she looks up at you with big heartbroken eyes just makes you feel sorry for her.

Years later, I can be much more precise regarding the reason for my personal devotion to Saint Mary Magdalene. This woman, out of whom Jesus cast seven demons, who is generally supposed to have been a prostitute; this woman of whom much was forgiven because she loved much, this woman was the first to see the risen Lord (Jn 20:11-18)! The opening prayer of the Mass of her feast states that Jesus "... first entrusted to Mary Magdalene the joyful news of His resurrection," and the gospels tell us she was sent to Peter and the disciples to announce the resurrection to them. For this, she bears the honorable title, Apostle to the Apostles.

What does that say? I think that it speaks to Jesus' respect for women in general, but in particular, I think that it speaks to the powerful love and devotion that Mary Magdalene held for Jesus from the time he healed her. Among the women who followed Jesus during his public ministry, Mary Magdalene is always mentioned first (Lk 8:2). From the gospels we know that she was an eyewitness to the crucifixion (Mt 27:56; Mk 15:40, Jn 19:25), was present at the burial of Jesus (Mt 27:61, Mk 15:47) and was at the empty tomb (Mt 28:1-10, Mk 16:1-8, Lk 24:1-12). Such representation in the gospels clearly demonstrates that her penitence was sincere and real.

St. Gregory the Great admonished his congregation on the feast of Mary Magdalene to reflect on Mary's attitude and the great love she felt for Christ; for though the disciples had left the tomb, she remained. She was still seeking the One she had not found, and while she sought, she wept; burning with the fire of love, she longed for Him who she thought had been taken away. And so it happened that the woman who stayed behind to seek Christ was the only one to see Him.

Whenever I feel like I can't do anything right, I think of Mary Magdalene who was forgiven much because she loved much. She stands as a witness to what is possible for those who seek Jesus' forgiveness. She stands as a witness of what is possible for you and for me.

# SHALOM

One of my favorite Gospel stories is the account of the healing of the hemorrhaging woman. This story, found in Mark's Gospel (Mk 5: 25-34) tells of a woman who had been afflicted by a hemorrhage for twelve years. She tried all different kinds of doctors and treatments, used up all of her money in the process and remained sick. In desperation she figured that if she could just touch the hem of Jesus' cloak, that would be enough; she would be healed. She took the chance, sneaked up on Him in the jostling crowd, touched the hem of His cloak and was healed. Jesus, however, realized that healing power had gone out from Him and whirled about in the crowd seeking the culprit. She came forward trembling, realizing that sooner or later He was going to find her out. But instead of chastising her, Jesus spoke the healing words: *"Daughter, your faith has saved you. Go in peace and be cured of your affliction."* (Mk 5:34).

In order to appreciate the beautiful message of this healing, we have to understand certain contextual nuances. First, we have to appreciate why she would have to sneak up on Jesus rather than just coming out and asking for healing. According to the Jewish ceremonial law, anyone coming into contact with blood was rendered unclean and could not come into contact with others lest they be made unclean as well. This woman had been excluded from all contact with other human beings for twelve years. Think about how many times each day we touch another person — in a hug, a handshake or just bumping into them in a crowded elevator. Touching is such an integral part of human life. Yet, the hemorrhaging woman was completely cut off from society — cut off from living a fully human life. They would never have allowed her to approach Jesus. By touching even His garment she would have made Him unclean as well, and so, of course, she must have been paralyzed with fear when He turned about in the crowd to find the one who had touched Him.

But instead of reprimand, the woman found gentleness, compassion and healing. Jesus called her daughter, welcoming her back into society. He sent her off with the greeting of peace — Shalom — which means being whole, being fully human, being free.

Take a moment to read the gospel story of the Hemorrhaging Woman. Imagine how lonely, how desperate, how hopeless the hemorrhaging woman must have felt, how ashamed, how excluded. Each of us has some area in our lives of which we are ashamed: some little secret that we just know would make everyone hate us if they knew; some little detail that keeps us bound in chains of guilt and anguish when we think about it. I like to think of the hemorrhaging woman as a teacher. She teaches us about taking chances. Because she had the courage to approach the Lord for healing, we learn that we can too.

The Christian life is not about being twisted up in guilt

about our mistakes and imperfections. We all make mistakes, and none of us is perfect. If perfection were the requirement for admission to church, we would have a lot of empty buildings. But Jesus does not demand perfection. He asks only that we consistently try our very best to live according to God's law of love.

I look at the hemorrhaging woman as a pioneer. She is a trail blazer. She has taken the risk out of approaching the Lord. Now that we have seen what was possible for her, we can take the chance of bringing our wounds, whatever they may be, to Jesus. We can lay them at the foot of the cross, have the courage to touch the hem of His garment and let Him heal us. We can feel His Shalom wash over us like a cool, refreshing breeze on a steamy August afternoon.

Let go of your fear. Let Jesus make you whole. Dare to be set free.

# 3

# DIVINE
# PROVIDENCE

*Cast all your worries upon him because he cares for you. (1Peter 5:7)*

Grove at Baughman's Rock, Ohiopyle State Park, Fayette County, Pennsylvania. Photo by Philip M. Kanfush, O.S.B.

# ORDER OUT OF CHAOS

Have you ever had one of those weeks where one thing after another went wrong? Of course you have; we all have. Often when we're having one of those weeks, or one of those months, or even one of those years, it can be hard not to get really down on ourselves and even become angry and bitter with God. It happens to everyone.

Once when I was a teenager, I was visiting my aunt. I was going through what I considered to be a terrible crisis. I was having a horrible struggle with algebra, I had tried out for the volleyball team but didn't make the squad, I had messed up my audition in concert band so I didn't get to play the part I had hoped for and the girl I had a crush on didn't know I was alive. Nothing seemed to be going right for me. Of course now I recognize how trivial it all was, but at the time the situation seemed dire.

My aunt was baking cookies while I bemoaned my adolescent tragedy. I now realize that she was a very wise woman because she taught me a powerful lesson that day. Finally, when she had endured as much of my drama as I suppose she could bear, she pointed out the ingredients that were spread across her kitchen table. She told me, "Look at these things." She pointed out the bottle of vanilla extract, the eggs, the shortening and flour each in turn, saying, "None of these things by themselves tastes very good." She continued, as she removed a tray of cookies from the oven, "It seems strange though. When you mix them all together and turn up the heat, they turn into these tasty cookies. Life has a way of working out in just this same way."

My aunt was a woman of deep faith. She understood that although we often wonder why God would let us go through rough times, He can take the chaos that we wreak in our lives and make it turn out just fine. Saint Paul writes: *We know that all things work for good for those who love God, who are called according to his purpose.* (Rom. 8:28). I guess this is what my aunt was trying to teach me that day.

Elsewhere, in his second letter to Timothy, Saint Paul calls to the Christian community, to you and to me, to... *bear your share of hardship for the gospel with the strength that comes from God. He saved us and called us to a holy life, not according to our works but according to his own design* (2Tim 1:8-9).

How can we have this ingrained and abiding trust? The answer seems to me to be locked deep within the context in which we live our lives.

When I attended the funeral of my brother-in-law's mother, her minister made a very good point — one that I often think about. The minister was talking about making sense of the bad things that happen in life and he pointed out that for us as Christians, things in life make sense because we live in a context of hope.

Think about it. Everything we do in life — all our attitudes, our choices, our whole approach to existence —is predicated on a belief that we are going to heaven – that there is a King-dom and that we are destined for everlasting life there. This basic premise of our philosophical anthropology is really the belief in the resurrection of Jesus Christ and the promise that we, too, will be raised on the last day. God does have a plan for us. Our conviction in His plan of salvation is the one belief that undergirds and sustains all the other tenets of our faith – of our whole life.

Think about my aunt's lesson. Does it help to make sense of the little or large catastrophes in your life? Can you let go and trust God to make order out of the chaos?

# THE MASTER'S RETURN

Advent is my favorite of the liturgical seasons. It always has been. When I was younger, I never really understood the reason, but as I grow older, and perhaps because of my monastic and seminary training, I better understand the reason. It is the beauty of the hymns, Scripture readings and prayers of the Advent season that so eloquently speak to the deepest longings of the human heart — to the deepest longings of my heart.

It wasn't until I came to live at the monastery that the full treasure trove of Advent beauty was revealed to me. The monk is schooled to live his life in a constant vigil of anticipation, awaiting the Master's return. He is trained to look at the world from his inner eye to recognize and revel in the countless manifestations of God's saving action in the merest details of every day life.

The monastic evening prayer is a great tool for the monk in helping him to enter into the beautiful promise of the Advent season. The antiphons we sing at evening prayer each day form for me the grist for the mill of my meditation during these days. As each day grows shorter, I find myself slowing down when the bells ring to summon us to evening prayer, calming my troubled mind and entering deeply into the Advent spirit so pregnant with hope.

Reflect on some of these antiphons: *Drop down dew, you heavens, from above, and let the clouds rain the Just: let the earth be opened and bud forth a Savior;* or *People of Zion, behold the Lord shall come to save the nations and the Lord shall make the glory of His voice to be heard, in the joy of your heart;* and especially my personal favorite, *See, your King comes, the master of the earth; he will shatter the yoke of our slavery.* When I hear the organ strike the melody for this antiphon, I am reminded of God's saving action for the Israelites and how he led them out of their slavery. I hear echo in my heart the reassurance He gave them through Moses when they were troubled and afraid: *But do not be afraid of them. Rather, call to mind what the LORD, your God, did to Pharaoh and to all Egypt: the great testings which your own eyes have seen, the signs and wonders, His strong hand and outstretched arm with which the LORD, your God, brought you out. The same also will he do to all the nations of whom you are now afraid.* (Deut 7: 18-19). These words refer in a concrete way to a specific intervention on God's part in history; but they also apply by metaphor to what He stands ready to do for each of us in our difficulties and problems. These are no mere words. This is a real promise to you and me. Which of us has not seen God work wonders in our lives? But we need to take time to remember so that we might be comforted and have hope. I always request that the hymn *O Come, O Come, Emmanuel* be sung at our Sunday Masses during Advent. Sing it or at least read along in your hymnal. Hear the words, remember the history, bask in the promise and make it your Advent prayer.

I usually find myself hurried and anxious with all of the rush of preparations for Christmas — the decorating, the shopping, the baking, the writing of cards — not to mention the frenetic and, frankly, chaotic pace of the closing of the fall semester in the College with its last ditch effort to cram in just one more lecture, exams to write, read and grade. But then I remember the promise behind the antiphons and I feel some moments of respite from the break-neck speed with which we all find ourselves driven to get more accomplished in less time.

Many years ago, there was a bulletin stuffer at my local church that talked about the speed of our lives. I clipped out the prayer at the end of the article and saved it. It's dulled and yellowed with the years, but I still pray it. As you find yourself feeling rushed, take a moment to reflect on the antiphons I've shared with you, on the hymn, *O Come, O Come, Emmanuel* that we've been singing, and pray this prayer, written  by Wilferd A. Peterson:

*Slow me down, Lord. Ease the pounding of my heart by the quieting of my mind. Remind me each day that there is more to life than increasing its speed. Let me look into the branches of the towering trees and know that they grew straight and strong because they grew slowly and well.*

# THE WAY OF PRUDENCE

When the fall semester has ended and the students have all gone home, the air is cold in the evening twilight, and an expectant hush falls over the countryside. A pregnant stillness lays all about. There is a feeling of waiting, of keeping vigil. The mood of the monks has become more solemn. At our Evening Prayer, we begin to sing the "O" antiphons — so named because they each begin with the word "O". We sing a different one each day until Christmas Eve.

During my first Advent in the monastery, the "O" antiphons seemed to be a great, holy mystery. First of all, they were ancient, dating from the 8th and 9th centuries. They seemed mysterious because we had to learn to chant them according to the Gregorian tones using Latin. They have such a haunting melody. They speak of the desperate longing of God's people for His return – and evoke at once both the Old Testament experience of the exile and the young Church's anxious expectation of Jesus' return in glory.

I think that part of their mystery is that each of these antiphons is prayed only once each year. They are deep, powerful supplications, each calling out to Christ by one of his ancient titles. On December 17th, we'll pray, *O Wisdom, you came forth from the mouth of the Most High, and reaching from beginning to end, you ordered all things mightily and sweetly. Come, and teach us the way of prudence!* Then on December 18th: *O Adonai and Rule of the house of Israel, you appeared to Moses in the fire of the burning bush, and on Mount Sinai gave him your Law. Come, and with an outstretched arm redeem us!* For December 19th: *O Root of Jesse, you stand for an ensign of mankind; before you kings shall keep their silence, and to you all nations shall have recourse. Come, save us, and do not delay.* On December 20th: *O Key of David and Scepter of the house of Israel; you open and no man closes; you close and no man opens. Come, and deliver him from the chains of prison who sits in darkness and in the shadow of death.* December 21: *O Rising Dawn, Radiance of the Light eternal and Sun of Justice; come, and enlighten those who sit in darkness and in the shadow of death.* December 22nd: *O King of the Gentiles and Desired of all, you are the cornerstone that binds two into one. Come, and save poor man, whom you fashioned out of clay.* And finally, on December 23rd: *O Emmanuel, our King and Lawgiver, the Expected of nations and their Saviour; Come, and save us, O Lord our God!*

These beautiful prayers do not belong to the monastic tradition alone. They are yours, too. Consider the great things that God has done in history, the great things He has accomplished in your life. Make ready to welcome Him into your heart and your home.

# PARADISE REOPENED

A traditional Christmas folk play opens with Mary and Joseph huddled together in a cold barn, near where Jesus lay in the manger. They hear a knock at the door. Joseph opens the door to find an old, tired-looking couple.

When they ask if they can see the child, Mary says "yes." They slowly make their way to the manger and look at the child. Then the old woman reaches under her shawl and puts a small object into the manger. Suddenly, the man and woman look much younger, more youthful, and more radiant and they dance for joy. Joseph and Mary look into the manger to see Jesus holding a small apple. They realize that the old man and the old woman were Adam and Eve, returning to God the apple, what they had taken from the Garden. It is a moment of forgiveness, one of reconciliation.

So often in the excitement of the Christmas season we fail to celebrate it in its fullness! For the birth of Christ is not a starting point for redemption history; salvation history begins with Adam and Eve. I love this stable story because it reminds us that Adam and Eve had a stake in the birth of Christ, too.

Legend has it that Adam and Eve wandered the earth waiting and searching for the savior promised them when they were banished from the Garden. Saint Ephrem the Syrian knew of this tradition when he composed his seventh hymn on the Nativity: *Blessed is the Babe who restored Adam's youth; he was displeased to see that he grew old and wasted away, yet the serpent who killed him shed [his skin] and recovered his youth. Blessed is the Babe by whom Eve and Adam were restored to youth.* And later, in his thirteenth hymn, *today let Eve rejoice in Sheol, for behold the Son of her daughter as the Medicine of Life came down to save the mother of His mother — the blessed Babe Who will crush the head of the serpent that wounded her.* The prayer of the Maronite tradition reminds us that *Adam's sin is canceled by the crying of a child.*

It is good to get excited when Christmas rolls around, but let us not fail to marvel in the Mystery which weaves together the whole of human history, for it is my story and yours. We, too, are rescued by the birth of the Christ child. All of our human possibilities are realized in the stable at Bethlehem. We are set free — free of the tyranny of sin; recreated in God's image, delivered from all that enslaves us, if we choose to accept that freedom. It would be a wonderful family tradition to place an apple ornament in your home's manger scene or on your Christmas tree to remind you that Paradise is reopened and death is merely a stable door.

# SPYING ON SANTA

Every family has Christmas traditions. These ultimately become the stuff of which memories are made. One of my family's
best traditions was the way we organized our presents under the
Christmas tree. Each of us had a pile of wrapped gifts there from
Mom and Dad, our grandparents and godparents. These would
already be in place before we were tucked in bed on Christmas
Eve. Our piles were arranged in order of age, with mine to the
extreme left, and Dad's on the far right. Though I knew some
families whose toys from Santa Claus came wrapped, in our
house it was different. There was a clear distinction between
what Santa brought and the other gifts we received. Because
he has a keen eye and recognized an orderly system already in
place beneath the tree, Santa Claus would neatly arrange the
toys he brought in front of our wrapped gifts. He knew that
my Mom was not about to tolerate chaos with six little ones to
manage on Christmas morning. And so it was that we each had
our own personal territory under the Christmas tree, where we
would find our toys on Christmas morning.

Like any other kids, we were always up well before the crack
of dawn when Christmas Day finally arrived. But Mom never al-

lowed us to go downstairs until seven o'clock. So we would all stealthily tiptoe up the attic stairs to the room where my oldest sister, Denise, slept, and gather there speculating in whispers and hushed voices as to what we might find beneath the tree. Denise would always sneak downstairs under the guise of needing a glass of water from the kitchen. Like a bounty hunter after prey, she'd stalk all the way down to the living room while we waited anxiously for her report. And when finally she returned to her attic lair, usually forgetting to bring the tell-tale glass of water for her alibi, we pounced on her for news of what she had observed in our piles during her reconnaissance mission.

In time I came to realize, that like all Christmas traditions, Denise could be counted on. Each year we would meet in the attic bedroom and deploy her on the annual espionage campaign, and from year to year, Denise was completely reliable. She saw baby dolls; she saw coloring books; she saw toy china sets; she saw Barbie stuff; she saw games that girls would want to play, but never, never once, did Denise manage to notice anything that was in my pile. I always had to wait until seven o'clock to find out what Santa had brought for me.

When the waiting is over and Christmas is upon us, we need to reflect on the feast of the Incarnation. Do we recognize it for what it truly is? Do we realize what Christ has brought for us? It is Christ's coming among us as man that makes possible our redemption — our eternal life. It is Christ abiding with us that sets us free, that gives us hope, that lifts whatever burdens our hearts. At midnight Mass we hear from the prophet Isaiah: *The people who walked in darkness have seen a great light; upon those who dwelt in the land of gloom a light has shone ... the yoke that burdened them, the pole on their shoulder, and the rod of their taskmaster you have smashed ... for a child is born to us, a son is given us; upon his shoulder dominion rests. They name him Wonder-Counselor, God-Hero, Father-Forever, Prince of Peace.* (Isaiah 9: 1, 3, 5) Rejoice! You need no longer live in gloom, enslaved by whatever grieves your heart. Cast off your yoke and be free! And rejoice! Rejoice! Rejoice! For today is born our Savior, Christ the Lord!

# GOD'S LOVE IS MANIFEST

Shortly after Christmas, I visited with a friend of mine. He made a comment about how his family was in the midst of taking down their Christmas decorations. He observed that it is depressing to clear Christmas away.

It seems to me that it is perfectly normal for us to feel a little let down or disappointed when we begin to pack up after the holidays. After all, we spent four weeks, liturgically speaking, to prepare for the Christmas Season, which lasts such a short time.

Then, we find ourselves carefully wrapping away our delicate decorations and our treasured memories acquired in Christmases past. It is natural to wonder what happened to the fellowship, the joy and the hope that we so carefully tended like budding poinsettias in a greenhouse during the weeks leading up to Christmas. As life slowly settles back to normal, we find ourselves wondering what that effort was all about.

The answer's simple. It is all about love – God's love for us. That's the whole story, plain and simple. Genesis tells us that in the beginning, after God had created all the beauty that surrounds us – all the beauty that we often take for granted – God created humankind. We are the crown of creation, His joy. He walked with us, personally present to Adam and Eve, and when they turned from Him, unwilling to return love for love, God still did not turn from us.

Again and again He sent prophets to cajole humankind to return His love, and when the time was right, He walked again among us. Born as one of us into a situation of poverty and pain so that He might make holy every last aspect of our existence, the messy along with the joyful, God continued to show His love for us.

That's what all the fuss we call Christmas is about. Is all the rushing around to get ready for so short a holiday season worth the trouble? I'd say so. It's never really over. *God is love* (1 Jn 4:16). Every time we do a kindness to another, we manifest that Love which called us — each of us personally — into existence. We don't have to do great acts, though perhaps some among us might. We just have to allow Him to be reflected in us by being the image of Him that we were created to be.

If you feel let down after some big event like Christmas, try doing a little act of kindness. Extend yourself that someone else might feel a spark of joy, and that God's love might be manifest.

I vividly remember my first year in the monastery. Arriving on July 1st full of excitement and hope for a new way of life, I expected it to be difficult. As novices, we're cloistered — we aren't allowed to leave the monastery grounds for a whole year. The first half of the year, from July through December, was easy enough, because as each day unfolded we learned a new aspect of what it means to be a monk. The novices' first Christmas in the monastery is beautiful and exciting, but the weeks after Christmas are the hardest. January and February seem to drag on forever. It seems like spring will never come and one quickly becomes downhearted. That's the time when we novices most needed encouragement that we were doing the right thing. A couple of cards I got during that time really made a difference for me.

Take a moment to send a note of encouragement to someone you know. It doesn't have to be elaborate, just buy a card and jot a line or two to let that person know that you're thinking of him or her. That simple act of kindness will make a difference in the recipient's life, and you will be blessed too. *The one who loves another has fulfilled the law* (Rom 13:8).

# PROMISE LOCKED IN A SEED

During May, the month which the Church dedicates to Mary, the Mother of God, I find myself reflecting on some of the little-known titles under which Mary is honored. One of the less recognized titles by which Mary is venerated is that of Our Lady of the Seeds. This title is celebrated in the Maronite Catholic tradition on May 15. It arises from a very ancient Middle Eastern custom.

There are three important agricultural feasts in the Maronite tradition: one for the planting of the seeds, one for the harvest of the wheat and a third for the harvest of the grapes. These commemorate the three farming actions that provide the bread and wine for the Eucharist.

According to the Maronite Synaxarion for the feast of Our Lady of the Seeds, its origin is *an agricultural feast which arose from the needs of the farmers to seek God's help for a fruitful harvest.* In the Middle East where conditions are so arid, *the farmers were at the mercy of the elements and depended upon sufficient rain and good weather. As a result, they sought God's assistance and begged the intercession of Mary for their crops.*

*The ancient texts speak of Mary's protection, not only in mate-*

*rial terms of the crops of the field, but also of her role in the Incarnation as the Mother of the Source of Life, Jesus Christ. Saint Ephrem speaks of Mary in this regard when he says that Mary became the field who received the grain of wheat in her womb and this grain of wheat, Jesus Christ our Lord, gives life to the world. Through the harvest we receive the gifts of bread and wine which become for us the body and blood of Christ in the Eucharist.*

Always mindful of this and of Mary's unique role in our salvation, the Maronite liturgy requires the priest to process with the bread and wine at the offertory while the people sing this beautiful hymn:

*I am the Bread of Life, said our Lord. From on high, I came to earth, so all might live in Me. Pure Word without flesh, I was sent from the Father. Mary's womb received Me like good earth a grain of wheat. Behold, the priest bears Me aloft to the altar. Alleluia! Accept our offering.*

Here at Saint Vincent, we have had the longstanding tradition of blessing the wheat when the first harvest of the year arrives at our Gristmill. When I first came here, we celebrated that blessing on the Feast of the Assumption, a tremendous feast celebrating Mary's role in salvation history. As always, our veneration of Mary points to her Son, whom we praise in and through Mary's obedient and loving discipleship. Reflection on her life shows us what is possible for all of us.

So often, we lose sight of our dependence on God's benevolent generosity, even in the simplest and most mundane aspects of our lives like planting seeds. Most of us plant gardens or flower beds about our homes in spring and summer. They create a beauty all around us that speaks a subtle word to our souls of God's own beauty, reflected in all of creation — a beauty in which we share, as the crown of creation.

Plant some seeds. But do not fail to offer a prayer to Mary, asking her to intercede on our behalf, that we might not lose sight of all the beauty around us, of the gift of the earth's bounty and of the promise, locked in a dry little seed, of the beautiful life that is possible for each of us. See in that seed an icon of the resurrection and the promise of the beauty that is eternal life — a beauty we cannot begin to fathom — that is possible for us because Mary said 'yes' to God's will in her life and showed us that we can say 'yes' too.

# GOD'S EMBROIDERY

When I was little, I remember that my mother used to spend a lot of time doing embroidery. For the most part she worked to decorate pillow cases and other linens. The pink and gray tin in which her embroidery flosses were kept was always a kind of mystery to me. I also wondered about how she worked the hoops. These things were always on the third shelf in the hall closet upstairs, but sometimes in the evening after dinner, she'd pull them out and sit down to sew. I don't know if anyone even does that anymore, but I hope that it has not become a lost art now that there are sewing machines that can do these things for us at a much greater rate of speed.

I recall that I used to sit there and play or read and watch her sew. Periodically, my mother would pause to turn the cloth over to inspect her work from the underside. I can remember being confounded about how the picture on the top looked so nice, while the underside was a messy hodgepodge of threads. I couldn't figure out why it didn't look the same on both sides.

It seems to me that there's a powerful lesson to be gleaned from the simple act of embroidery and my childhood confusion about it. This lesson is twofold. On the one hand, I believe that it teaches us about the power of perception in our human interactions. So often, when we see someone doing something, it makes no sense to us at all. We like to think that we know what we would do or say in a given situation, and very frequently, our way would be quite different from what we observe. However, we can never be fully aware of others' motivations. All we can know, epistemologically speaking, is what we are able to perceive with our five senses. The problem is that information gathered through our senses is seldom complete, particularly as it relates to the behavior of other people. Our senses cannot tell us anything about the path that the other individual has walked and the experiences that have led him to the behavior that we see and find ourselves judging in the present. All we really see, as it were, is a hodgepodge of threads – a mixed jumble. What we don't see is the picture from the other's perspective. That is the reason we must be very careful not to give in to the temptation to draw conclusions about other people. Some of the threads in their lives may be beautiful and bright, but others may be somber and dark. All of these threads put together make a picture we can never truly see. The lesson to be learned from the art of embroidery is not to make rash judgments about others.

On the other hand, the same can be said about our relationship with God. His actions in our lives can seldom be seen in their proper perspective. When things are going well for us and we are very happy, it is easy to trust in God's Providence. When they are going poorly and we find ourselves dissatisfied, it's quite a different story. We believe that God has a plan. The scriptures demonstrate how it has unfolded in salvation history from Adam to the present. That's the big plan. It is easy to have faith in that. But our loving Father also has a plan for each of us.

That's the plan that is hard to see and even harder to trust. Some of the threads are joyful and colorful; others may seem dark and gloomy. But sometimes, like my mother's embroidery, we can only see what appears to be a tangled mess.

When we're going through a dark period in our lives, we need to call to mind that our Father loves us. These dark threads, which so often arise from our own poor choices, can have a meaning and purpose that is just as important in forming the beautiful picture that He has planned for us as those that seem brighter. Faith calls us to trust and to remain open to the Spirit at work in our lives. In the book of Proverbs we read:

*Trust in the LORD with all your heart,*
  *on your own intelligence rely not;*
*In all your ways be mindful of him,*
  *and he will make straight your paths* (3:5-6).

If you're anything at all like me, some days all you can do is to trust. Try never to lose hope in the fact that the mess you see from your side of God's embroidery hoop is a beautiful scene from His perspective, and trust.

# A SEASON FOR CHANGE

As I write, autumn has definitely come. The leaves are turning brilliant shades of gold, red and copper, fluttering gracefully on the branches, and wafting lazily to the ground on the gentle fall breezes. The flowers bloom with less and less enthusiasm. But as the plant world is slowing down, the animals are gearing up for winter. Squirrels and chipmunks scurry to and fro with cheeks bulging, and at my bird feeder, the finches have begun to lose their orange and red plumage for their dull brown winter coats.

In human society, we, too, begin to prepare for winter. Furnaces are being overhauled, screens are coming out of windows, and like the finches, our heavy coats and winter clothes are coming out of storage. It is a season for change.

Our lives go through seasons of change too. And lately I've been working with people who are growing through very different seasons of life. What I have seen is that change can be difficult, frustrating and even painful. But that doesn't necessarily make change a bad thing -- especially those changes that come about as a result of the natural rhythms of our life cycles.

It seems to me, as I begin to enter into my own season of

mid-life, that perhaps part of the reason that we resist change so much is that we are afraid. Perhaps we're afraid our summer season was not as fruitful as it should have been, or maybe we are afraid that we won't accomplish everything we want to. Maybe we're afraid because we don't know what will happen to us next. But we don't need to be afraid. We do not go through the seasons of our life alone. No matter what kind of change we might be experiencing in our lives at present, we can be at peace. The Lord himself tells us, *"Be brave and steadfast; have no fear or dread of them, for it is the LORD, your God, who marches with you; he will never fail you or forsake you"* (Dt. 31:6).

Reflect on a change that is taking place in your life. Can you see the Spirit present? In your prayer, reflect on this Scripture verse from Deuteronomy and ask the Lord to help you to recognize his presence in your life.

# HIS HAND IS PRESENT

From the time of my boyhood, Holy Week has been my favorite time of the liturgical year. The prayers and hymns of the special liturgies speak to my heart in a particularly strong way. Among the most powerful of the hymns is the Reproaches which used to be sung during the Veneration of the Cross at the Good Friday service. I haven't heard the Reproaches sung in many years; other hymns are more often sung these days, but with their poignant refrain, *My people, what have I done to you? How have I offended you? Answer me!* the Reproaches still plumb the depths of my soul, and provide fodder for reflection as I move through Holy Week.

In the Reproaches the Eastern and the Western traditions meet as one, praying together the powerful Trisagion: *Holy is God! Holy and Strong! Holy immortal One, have mercy on us!* Who among us can remain unmoved as we hear the voice of Jesus cry out to us in the Reproaches?

*I led you out of Egypt, from slavery to freedom,*
*but you led your Savior to the cross.*

*I led you on your way in a pillar of cloud,*
*but you led me to Pilate's court.*

*I bore you up with manna in the desert,*
*but you struck me down and scourged me.*

*I gave you a royal scepter,*
*but you gave me a crown of thorns.*

*I raised you to the height of majesty,*
*but you have raised me high on a cross.*

*My people, what have I done to you?*
*How have I offended you? Answer me!*

Holy Week is a very emotional time for me for another reason as well. It was during my visit to the Archabbey back in 1993 when I finally accepted the Lord's call in my life. I vividly remember sitting on the steps of Leander Hall after the Mass of the Lord's Supper that Holy Thursday evening and praying more fervently than I had ever prayed in my whole life. It was a balmy April evening, probably close to 70 degrees, and the moon was full, hanging low in the night sky. I sat there thinking about the first Passover, envisioning the full moon shining over Egypt, trying to fathom God's saving action in the lives of a rag-tag hoard of slaves — poor, dispossessed, hopeless people. And I thought about how God had worked in my life and about the opportunity He was offering to me, unworthy as I am. All my life I had been hiding from this vocation. I knew that I had been called to the religious life and to the priesthood from the time

I was a very small boy, but by the time that I was old enough to act on that call, I no longer felt good enough. That night as I sat in the moonlight, feeling the weight of a half a lifetime of sometimes questionable choices, I felt the Lord speaking to my heart in spite of my unworthiness. Through the working of some extraordinary grace, I knew deep within the recesses of my broken heart that God had not given up on me, that I had not messed things up too badly, and that I could still come to live the life I had been born to live. And so the next morning, I sought out the Vocation Director and told him that if it wasn't too late, I wanted to accept his invitation to begin the application process for the Archabbey's novitiate. That Easter Sunday, after the family dinner, I told my parents that I was applying to enter the monastery.

Except when I was stationed as a Deacon in Carrolltown during Holy Week, I have never failed to return briefly to the steps of Leander Hall after Mass on Holy Thursday to offer my thanks to God for the gift of my vocation and to marvel anew at the work He has wrought in salvation history. There I reflect again on the Reproaches, keeping my own silent vigil with Him as if in the Garden, and asking my Lord once more to accept my service in all its brokenness.

Reflect upon the Reproaches. Consider how the Lord has worked in your own life. No matter what your circumstances, His hand continues to be present to guide and strengthen you. Give thanks for those blessings you have received so freely from His hand, and for those times when you may have squandered His gifts; join me in praying the Trisagion: *Holy is God, Holy and Strong! Holy immortal One, have mercy on us!* — and on the whole world. May God speak to your heart during these high holy days.

# 4
# POWER MADE PERFECT

*…My grace is sufficient for you, for power is made perfect in weakness (2Cor 12:9).*

Ohiopyle Falls, Ohiopyle State Park, Fayette County, Pennsylvania.
Photo by Philip M. Kanfush, O.S.B.

# NO COWARDLY SPIRIT

My monastic community has been reading from the book of Esther at our morning prayer. It's one of my favorite stories. The book tells how a young Jewish woman, through a courage born of her faith, saves the Israelites from destruction.

For me, the most inspiring part of the story is when Esther prays to God for assistance in her struggle to save her people. The story tells us she prayed to the Lord, the God of Israel, saying: *'My LORD, our King, you alone are God. Help me, who am alone and have no help but you. Be mindful of us, O LORD. Manifest yourself in the time of our distress, and give me courage, King of gods and Ruler of every power. Put in my mouth persuasive words in the presence of the lion. O God, more powerful than all, hear the voice of those in despair. Save us from the power of the wicked, and deliver me from my fear'* (In the N.A.B. version, C:14,23- 24, 30.)

Esther teaches me how to pray when I need to have courage. That's when I pull out my Bible and I make Esther's prayer my own. If we are honest with ourselves, we have to admit that we all experience times when our courage falters. Maybe we need to be brave about some medical condition that threatens us, or possibly we have to be strong about confronting someone in a damaged relationship. Perhaps courage is needed to stand up to a bully in some area of our life or to face our own brokenness. Some days we fret because we just don't know what's going to happen to us next. And each and every day we need to have the guts to stand up for our faith and gospel values – so Esther's prayer is for all of us.

We must not allow our worries to make us slaves to fear. We can confidently approach God when we are afraid. Saint Paul reminds us, *You did not receive a spirit of slavery to fall back into fear, but you received a spirit of adoption, through which we cry, "Abba, Father!"* (Rom 8:15).

Pray for courage to face whatever is troubling you in your life. Be strong. Take some time to read the Book of Esther — it is less than ten pages. Pray Esther's prayer confidently, and rest assured: *For God did not give us a spirit of cowardice but rather of power and love and self-control* (2Tim 1:7).

# A NEW FIRE IN OUR EYES

When I was in college, one of my favorite singers was Pat Benatar. *Rolling Stone Magazine* has called her the most successful female hard rock singer of the Eighties. My friends and I blasted her music on our stereos in our dorm rooms for hours. We sang along to songs like "Love is a Battlefield," "Hit Me With Your Best Shot" and "Shadows of the Night" with all the enthusiasm and fervor that only teenagers have for wrestling life's cold, hard truths.

I came across a CD with Pat Benatar's hits. Surrendering to a wave of nostalgia, I bought the CD. One of the songs caught my attention because its words seemed to ring true in a different way for me now than they did when the song came out in 1988. The song, "All Fired Up," seems to talk about conversion – an odd thing to find in a hard rock hit. No doubt Ms. Benatar had something else in mind, but when I hear the song now, it seems to tell the story of my own journey toward becoming a monk and a priest. The song says:

*"Livin' with my eyes closed,*
*Goin' day to day.*
*I never knew the difference –*
*I never cared either way.*
*Lookin' for a reason, searchin' for a sign …*

*Now I believe there comes a time,*
*When everything just falls in line.*
*We live an' learn from our mistakes,*
*The deepest cuts are healed by faith.*
*Now I got a new fire,*
*Burnin' in my eyes*
*Lightin' up the darkness ...*
*All fired up."*

My faith journey – my process of conversion – is much like the situation described by these lyrics. Yours is too. The Church Fathers described our conversion according to what they called The Three Ways. We find ourselves going through life blindly, but then something happens to change us. We experience what the Christian tradition calls an Awakening, when we receive that sign that Benatar talks about. We begin to wise up, learning from our mistakes, and growing in our ability to trust God to heal us – our deepest cuts really are healed by faith. The spiritual masters call this the Purgative Way. After we've grown in trust, we find it easier and easier to live as the Gospel asks. This is the Illuminative Way, when we really do have a new fire burning in our eyes, lighting up the darkness – a time when we find ourselves all fired up. Finally, some among us are able to let go completely and give God total control of their lives living in what tradition calls the Unitive Way – in union with God, when everything just falls in line.

God calls each of us to work our way through our faith journey in a different way and at a different pace. Take a few moments to think about your journey of faith. Where do you see yourself? What still needs healing? Give it to the Lord in trust. Let Him say to you, as He does to the hemorrhaging woman, *Courage, daughter! Your faith has saved you* (Mt. 9:22).

# HAPPINESS IS THE WAY

The sister of a friend of mine had two open heart surgeries at age 26 and nearly died. She was hospitalized for nearly two months with a number of complications, both before and after the surgeries.

After that, my friend tells me, her boyfriend left her and she had to move back home to recuperate. It turned out that those surgeries were not only a life-saving experience, but a life-changing one. The recuperation took over six months, each day with its own bit of progress, or sometimes with a setback. At an age when most young people still live their lives as if they will live forever, my friend's sister learned a valuable lesson in facing and overcoming death.

As her recovery progressed, my friend noticed the delight her sister took in even the simplest things — a sunbeam filtering through the living room window, warming her face as she rested on the couch; the way the family dog took to following her everywhere, even waiting outside the bathroom door as she washed up; the simple act of sharing family meals together again. There were tense and trying moments as well. But somehow, things had changed. And, without their knowing it, the rest of the family had changed, too, growing to appreciate even the simplest tasks, especially those performed together.

My friend's sister went on to find a new boyfriend, marry and bear a son. But she never forgot what she learned in the hospital — she took delight in every day, she lived each day to the fullest and she never, ever failed to mention her new-found happiness to her family. She died six years later, at age 32.

One of the things that helped my friend get through that dark period in her life was her faith, another was the memory of the way her sister lived, each and every day.

When I find myself searching for God to help me "get through" things, I am reminded of the fact that God is not present to me in the past, so it's pointless looking back wistfully on a "better" day. God is not present to me in the future, for it has not yet been called into existence. I cannot know that when it comes to pass it will be "better." I can only know this: God is present to me now, right here in these circumstances in which I find myself in this moment of my journey. To recognize this truth and to live accordingly is true wisdom, true happiness.

*Happy the man who finds wisdom,*

*the man who gains understanding!* (Prov 3:13).

Take some time to ponder the mystery of God's presence in your life. Reflect on the lyrics of this hymn found in our *Breaking Bread* hymnal: *This day God gives me strength of high heaven, sun and moon shining, flame in my hearth, flashing of lightning, wind in its swiftness, deeps of the ocean, firmness of earth. This day God sends me Strength as my guardian, Might to uphold me, Wisdom as guide. Your eyes are watchful, Your ears are list'ning, Your lips are speaking, Friend at my side.* [Text ascribed to St. Patrick; adapted by James D. Quinn, S.J.]

# DO NOT BE AFRAID

In John's gospel, we read, *the Advocate, the holy Spirit that the Father will send in my name — he will teach you everything and remind you of all that [I] told you. Peace I leave with you; my peace I give to you. Not as the world gives do I give it to you. Do not let your hearts be troubled or afraid* (Jn 14:26-27). This reading means the Easter season is drawing to its close, and we are preparing for the celebration of Pentecost. We recall how the Father sent the Spirit upon the apostles gathered in the upper room. That was a special day, but the Lord continues to send the Spirit upon each of us — the Advocate to teach us and remind us of everything Jesus said; to bring us His peace.

May 20th, 2001, was the first anniversary of my ordination to the priesthood — a very special day in the life of my family. But May 20th is special in my family for another reason as well. It was on May 20th, 1996, that my niece Hanna died. Hanna had been born with a genetic anomaly that was, as the doctors told us at the time, incompatible with life. Simply put, this meant that Hanna could not live for long. We might have a few days, a few weeks, optimistically a couple months at the most. And so, without really talking about it at all, we set about loving Hanna in earnest — all of us. My parents, my sisters, their husbands and children all gathered around my sister Michaleen and her husband Scott to celebrate this gift of new life that was fragile and precious and bittersweet. So, we gathered as a family every single weekend to celebrate the gift of family during those two brief months. And all during this time, though I don't recall us talking specifically about it, I know that each and every member of my family, in his or her own way, was working very, very hard to remain open to the Spirit. We were heartbroken, and that's the truth, but we believed — with a desperate faith — that good would come of Hanna's life, if only we could remain open to the voice of the Spirit. We didn't understand why Hanna couldn't stay with us, yet we remained faithful, trusting that Hanna had many lessons to teach us, or rather, that God had many lessons to teach us in and through Hanna's life and death. We recognized through some extraordinary gift of grace that understanding was not essential — but that remaining faithful was. And so we remained faith-filled people — in spite of our pain, our anger, our fear, our resentment, our sadness — never becoming bitter.

Hanna, though born with original sin like all of us, was washed clean of that stain through her baptism. She is a saint forever. I, through the laying on hands and invocation of the Holy Spirit, am a priest forever. I believe that our destinies are intertwined — forever. Hanna's short little life and my experience of the Spirit during that time, shaped the character of my ministry — of my priesthood. I do not think it accidental that my ordination ended up scheduled for May 20th. I think that God has a special plan for Hanna and me. I'm not sure what it is, but when the time comes to apply what the Spirit taught me, I'm sure He'll let me know.

Reflect on your life. What is troubling you? Let it go. Trust that the Spirit, the Advocate, is with you to teach you all that the Lord wants you to know, and make a quiet space in your life to listen to His soft voice. But never, never lose hope. As Saint Paul reminds us, *we are afflicted in every way, but not constrained; perplexed, but not driven to despair; persecuted, but not abandoned; struck down, but not destroyed* (2Cor 4:8-9) and elsewhere, *we know that all things work for good for those who love God, who are called according to his purpose* (Rom 8:28).

# BY GOD'S ORDER

May 30 is the feast of Saint Joan of Arc. She was burned at the stake on May 30, 1431, having been found guilty on twelve charges relating to sorcery and heresy.

Joan of Arc is one of the saints to whom I have a particular devotion. This devotion developed through repeated exposure to her history at different points in my life. Her story fascinated me as a boy when I read about her in the library at St. Titus School in Aliquippa. When I was in high school, I studied Joan's life as it was portrayed in French culture. When I got to college, I attended Mass at Saint Paul Cathedral, where a life-sized statue of Joan kneeling with her armor appeared at a side altar. Many, many times during my college years I stopped at the cathedral and knelt to pray at her altar. So for me, Joan is an old and dear friend. I think we all can learn from her life.

Joan was an ordinary peasant girl, born in Domrémy, France. She was thirteen in 1425 when she first heard the "voices" which would guide her life and destiny. She first identified Saint Michael and later Saint Catherine of Alexandria and Saint Margaret as those who had been sent by God to be her counsel. *"Saint Michael, when he came to me, told me that Saint Catherine and Saint*

*Margaret would come to me and that I should act on their advice,*
*that they were instructed to lead and advise me in what I had to do;*
*and that I should believe in what they would say to me, for it was*
*by God's order."* [1] Gradually Joan came to understand the meaning of these visions and the mission God had given her. Her role,
impossible as it must have seemed to her, was to liberate France
from English domination and to assist the French prince to be
crowned King of France.

Today we would say that Joan was crazy, but she was exam-
ined by a group of theologians who found no fault with her simple faith, and was permitted to lead a French army. Against all
odds, Joan was successful. Ultimately, the prince was crowned as
King Charles VII. In a subsequent battle at Compiègne, Joan was
captured by the Burgundians who sold her to the English. The
English had her tried as a heretic and a witch. Joan's long and
arduous ecclesiastical trial was completely illegal and unfair
– it had been undertaken in utter disregard to Joan's appeal to
the Pope, and Joan was uneducated, with hardly the acumen to
defend herself against learned scholars from the University of
Paris. She was mistreated and abused, but her faith never wa-
vered. Joan was 19 years old when the English burned her alive.
Her only request was that a crucifix be held before her eyes.
They didn't even afford her the dignity of burial – Joan's ashes
were scattered in the Seine.

Certainly this brief synopsis of Joan's life does not do her
justice, but it provides enough background for some reflection
about the characteristics of this young woman – characteristics
that we can emulate. First among these virtues is Joan's simplicity. She wasn't educated; Joan simply believed what her voices
told her. Faith isn't about education. Faith is gift, plain and sim-

ple. It can grow through appropriate study, but knowledge does not make one more faith-filled. Joan's simplicity points to a pure faith, in spite of challenges from all sides, she just trusted – period. In our day, when women have equal rights and we have such a developed legal system, it is hard for us to imagine the raw courage that Joan must have possessed and the strength of faith and character that would have been necessary to enable her to face such an ordeal. Another aspect of Joan's life that can give us hope is the fact that even though all seemed lost for her, in the end she was vindicated.

When I look at Joan's life, I find myself wondering why I can't be more like her. Why do I second-guess God's will in my life; why can't I just trust more? When we commemorate Pentecost, when God sent the Spirit upon the Church, we need to be reminded that we have received a share of that Spirit – the same Spirit that worked in Joan's life to achieve God's will through her humble cooperation. Reflect on your own life. How is the Spirit working in you? In what areas do you need to work on trusting God's will more? Learn from Joan's example and pray with her:

*The LORD is my strength and my shield.*

*In whom my heart trusted and found help* (Ps 28:7).

[1] This is from her testimony on March 15, 1431. In MS 1119, this passage occurs on folio 37r, lines 33 - 37.

# THE LIGHT OF A NEW DAY

I'm writing this on Wednesday, September 12th, 2001. In New York and D.C. they're just beginning to try to dig out from under the rubble, and here I sit in my cozy, quiet office. Like many of you, my emotions have run the gamut in the past 24 hours: shock, disbelief, anger, horror, hopelessness, sadness, grief, nausea. Now I'm numb.

Most of us probably spent September 11th glued to our televisions and radios listening to reports, one more gruesome than the next. I didn't have access to a television until after 9 p.m., but we could get radio reports at the parish office, and folks called in to tell us what they were reporting on television.

For me, I guess the tragedy didn't sink in until I was walking through the garden on my way to the dean's office to lend my support to Campus Ministry's efforts. One of my students called to me from his dormitory window. He was a reservist and wanted to know what to do about his classes if his unit were to be called up. I did not know he was in the reserves. He was just a freshman, so young, but a real nice kid.

At the college, we held prayer in the Basilica from noon until 5 p.m. Then there was a Mass for Peace at 8 p.m. For our lunch break, the parish staff shut down the Parish Center and joined the college students in the Basilica for the rosary. Then I went over to the student union to see if I could be of help there, where a resource station manned by clergy and counselors was available to the students. It was pretty quiet there, so after a while, I went back to the office to place a call to Christ the Divine Teacher School to check on the school children. Since September 11th was the International Day of Peace (how ironic), they were getting ready to have their prayer service for peace as scheduled, but it had been moved indoors.

I went to the Mass for Peace in the evening. It was a beautiful, beautiful liturgy. Fr. Fred had a wonderful message and the Archabbot did too. What moved me most, however, was the number of college students who attended the liturgy and the fullness of their participation. It was moving, touching and comforting. It gave me hope to see our young people gather for prayer, and to pray so earnestly.

Again and again, the news reports made reference to how people all over America were seeking comfort in prayer and gathering in their churches. I take that as a sign of hope. We are never stronger than when we gather as the mystical body of Christ.

This morning at the weekday Mass, we sat somberly quiet for a few minutes, then I stood and pointed to the rose window of the Basilica that faces east. The sun was beginning to shine through it. "There is your sign", I said. "God has chosen to give us the light of a new day. This is our cause for hope." I am very deeply grieved by the evil caused by some dreadful, wicked people who have chosen to misuse the free will that God gave us so that we might seek Him. But I am equally inspired and hope-filled at the proper use of free will by all those who have turned out to support the relief effort by giving their time, talents and prayers. It gives glory to God.

We are sure saddened at this awful tragedy. But let us recall the words of Jeremiah:

*Remembering it over and over*
*leaves my soul downcast within me.*
*But I will call this to mind,*
*as my reason to have hope:*
*The favors of the LORD are not exhausted,*
*his mercies are not spent;*
*They are renewed each morning,*
*so great is his faithfulness.*
*My portion is the LORD, says my soul;*
*therefore I will hope in him.* (Lam 3:20-24).

# KEEP THE LORD BEFORE ME

In spite of the September 11th tragedy and our broken hearts, the American people began to resume their normal routines as much as possible. For my Organizational Behavior class, I felt a shot in the arm was necessary to raise spirits. I entered them in the Freshman Orientation Program's annual scavenger hunt. I sorted my 43 students into 6 teams, and we gathered at the Student Union at 9:30 p.m. to join the other nine teams entered in the competition. The prize was $100, and if one of my teams won, they earned 10 bonus points.

The teams first had to solve four clues in succession in order to locate the list numbering some 97 items to be scavenged. The items ranged from simple things like a dormitory room telephone to more exotic items like a member of the Saint Vincent Fire Department in full gear. As they located items, teams could return to the Student Union and deposit them at their team's table, but each time they chose to make a deposit, the team had to leave a member there to guard its treasure trove. Obviously, success would require planning and strategy.

The purpose of the scavenger hunt from the Orientation Program's point of view was no doubt to promote camaraderie and to help the students learn more about the campus. My purpose in using the scavenger hunt as a class activity was to give my students a hands-on opportunity to experience the development of work teams comprised of diverse individuals, particularly as task groups develop under time pressure (they only had one hour). My students then composed a brief paper describing their experience and analyzed the exercise in light of the theories of group formation and development we discussed in class. My hope was that my students had some sorely needed fun, and that the concepts I taught them might be retained at least until the day of the test.

I have to admit that this was the largest class I have had in my fifteen years of college teaching. But it was also the most congenial. Not one of these students gave me any trouble about coming out at 9:30 at night for a mandatory class activity. They were a joy to teach, and I don't know when I have enjoyed teaching more.

Life's been teaching us a lot of hard lessons lately. But even in the midst of our sadness, we can see that the basic joy that characterizes the American spirit is not daunted. Even though none of my students' teams won the Scavenger Hunt, for a couple of hours they relaxed and enjoyed each others' company, putting aside worry for play. I did too, and it was healing for my spirit to watch my students become more cohesive as a class and experience what I've taught them about group dynamics.

Continue to pray for all who have been affected by September 11th, but try to find some joy in the ordinary routines of your life. After all, God is with us in even the most mundane circumstances.

*I keep the LORD always before me;*

*with the LORD at my right, I shall never be shaken* (Ps 16:8).

# AN ANGEL BEFORE YOU

In the aftermath of the terrorist attack of September 11th, many people began to question how God could have let such a terrible act of violence be perpetrated on our nation. Much of the answer to that question comes down to the issue of our free will. I do not believe that God wills such things to happen. Quite to the contrary I believe that such acts of violence break God's heart. However, God does not directly interfere with choices and actions we take through His gift of our own free wills.

While God does not intervene directly in free will choices, we are never left bereft of His grace. Sometimes that grace comes in the form of the gentle inspirations we receive from His angels.

I have no doubt whatsoever that angels were very much involved doing God's work on September 11th. When we think about the devastation that could have happened in the attack, of the numbers who could potentially have been affected so drastically, it seems as if Divine Providence was indeed working to save lives and minimize the damage of so wicked a choice for evil.

One of the reasons I enjoyed the television show, *Touched By*

*An Angel,* so much is that I really do believe that angels work in our lives all the time. Maybe their efforts are not so overt as on the television show, and perhaps they'll never reveal their true identities to us, but I believe that angels do, in fact, move in our lives.

When we were little, we were taught to pray to our guardian angels each morning using a simple prayer which we probably forgot once we began to grow into adolescence. Maybe we need to start praying it again: *Angel of God, my guardian dear, to whom God's love entrusts me here, ever this day be at my side, to light and guard, to rule and guide.*

Start praying to your guardian angel again. Your angel can help to guide you in the right use of your free will if you remain open to his gentle promptings in your heart. Just as the angel never left Israel's side as it journeyed through the desert to the promised land, so your angel never leaves you alone. It is to you also that the Lord speaks, *See, I am sending an angel before you, to guard you on the way and bring you to the place I have prepared. Be attentive to him and heed his voice.* (Ex 23:20-21)

# A LESSON ABOUT LOVE

I once met a woman named Ella. I was working as a Financial Aid Director at the Community College of Allegheny County in Pittsburgh. Ella was a single mother. She had only one child, a son, whom she had named Joseph. I came to know them when Joseph applied to study at the College. He was eighteen years old and just graduated from high school.

It was very important to Ella that Joseph receive an education. He came to me when his application for federal student aid was denied. As I reviewed his application results, I realized that Joseph's application had not really been denied, it had been rejected because too much information was missing for the Department of Education to determine his eligibility. In the course of our interview, I discovered, not surprisingly for a new high school graduate, that Joseph had had no job and no income. I also came to recognize that like many young students, Joseph had no idea whatsoever what his mother's income was. So I gave him a questionnaire for his mother to complete that might shed some light on the needed information.

If anything at all could be said for young Joseph, it would

be that he was a man of great patience and perseverance. At least five times, he brought the questionnaire to me, each time without the needed information. Gauging from her responses on the forms, Ella had no income whatsoever. As the weeks wore on, the questions I gave him to take home to Ella became simpler and more direct. Finally, I was asking questions like, "do you own your home or do you rent?" The response came back that Ella rented their home. Then, I asked, "how much rent do you pay each month?" I no longer recall the exact amount she indicated, but I do remember that it was very low. Gradually, through an exhausting volley of questions and answers like this that grew to include inquiries about such items as the weekly grocery bill, and the electric and phone bills and from what sources they were paid, I hoped to get a handle on Ella's income so that I could complete Joseph's application for financial aid and get him enrolled. Each and every time, however, Ella's reported expenses were quite reasonable, but she maintained that her income was zero. Ella and I even had several telephone conversations about their financial situation, but she stalwartly maintained that she had no income. I could never allow Joseph to submit an application that indicated no family income because the government would assume that an error had occurred in the completion of the form. Even "in kind" support has a monetary value.

Finally, on one fateful morning, Ella accompanied Joseph to the Financial Aid Office to meet with me. I was not expecting her, but I was very glad to meet with her because I believed that finally the confusion could be resolved. What I did not imagine was that our brief encounter would touch me so profoundly that some fifteen years later, I can recall every detail.

Joseph waited in the hall while his mother and I met. As Ella faced me across my desk, I beheld the visage of a woman aged some twenty to thirty years beyond her chronological age. I surmised that life had not been easy for Ella. I pulled Joseph's file and began to ask her the same questions that she had already attempted to answer in the mountain of paper I had sent home with Joseph in the preceding weeks. After about fifteen minutes of pointless questions, Ella broke. With tears of shame trickling down her withered cheeks, Ella told me, "I will tell you how I get money, but you can't tell Joseph. Joseph can never know." I recall that a huge knot formed in my stomach as I pondered what to do in this situation. I was all of twenty-four years old. I did not know how to handle this. I imagined that she must be involved in something illegal and had no idea how I should handle whatever she might reveal to me. Meanwhile, I must have been staring at her with a blank look on my face, because Ella continued, "If Joseph found out what I do, he would hate me, and I can't have that, I just can't." She sobbed, "He's all I have."

I never let Ella tell me what she did to get the money she needed to keep a roof over her son's head and food in his belly. To do so would have been to allow her to disgrace herself before me unnecessarily, and I gathered that life had already shamed her more than enough. Instead, what I did was listen and learn. I listened to a story about a woman who had never known a decent opportunity in her life, a woman who had known only one joy, the son with whom she had discovered herself pregnant and abandoned, cast off mercilessly by her family. I heard the story of a woman who had named her son Joseph in the faithful hope that his fate might turn out as triumphantly as that of Jacob's son, "in the Bible, you know," Ella reminded me, as though I might never have read it.

And as I listened, I learned. I learned that dignity doesn't come from having fancy degrees. I learned that integrity doesn't come from having money. I learned that love is so powerful a force that it must be protected at all cost. I learned that grace comes even where opportunity is lacking, and perhaps precisely because opportunity is lacking. And in the face of this impoverished, broken woman whom life had beaten into gold, I felt exceedingly small.

On my drive home that evening I had an hour to reflect on Ella and Joseph. I came to understand the compassion that Jesus showed to the woman whose sins he forgave because she loved much. I came to recognize the incredible gift I had been given that day, and I cried.

With my meager help, Joseph did get to go to college, the first one in her family, Ella assured me proudly, to make such an achievement. Before the Christmas break that first semester, Joseph appeared at my office door. I thought something must be wrong. Everything was fine. His mother had sent him to bring me a Christmas card from the two of them. It was an inexpensive card, not really very pretty, but not surprisingly, it was my most prized gift that year. I do not know what happened to him and Ella, but I have never forgotten to pray for them. My prayer is that Joseph has overcome his poverty and become rich in money as well as grace. My prayer is that he has taken care of Ella and that her old age has been an easy one. I'll never know, but I pray for them all the same.

Ella's story teaches us a powerful lesson. So often in life we find ourselves confronted with what seem to be insurmountable difficulties and limitations. But if we take a careful look at them, I wonder if they really are so impossible to overcome?

Sometimes, when I'm feeling as though I can never succeed at something I'm trying to do, or that my plans will never work out, I have to stop and remind myself that the struggles I have to deal with are pretty insignificant compared to those of others. Most of us have it pretty easy in life when you stop to think about it. Perhaps we should stop every now and again to take stock of our problems. Are they really as bad as they seem, or like Ella, when life shovels dirt on us, can we learn to just shake it off and take a step up out of the hole in which we find ourselves?

Consider the story in Genesis of Joseph, Jacob's son. Though his brothers cast him in a cistern and left him for dead, he wound up second in command of the Pharaoh's dynasty.

*Comfort, give comfort to my people*
*says your God.*
*Every valley shall be filled in,*
*every mountain and hill shall be made low* (Is 40: 1, 4).

No matter how busy you are, you owe it to yourself to spend some moments allowing the Lord to fulfill His promise of comfort in your life. Then, take a moment to share that comfort with someone else.

# HOT SPOTS

I grew up in a region dominated by the steel industry, and had a college roommate who was a metallurgical engineering student, but it never occurred to me what I might have learned about life by being surrounded by people knowledgeable about how metal is formed until an artist friend of mine took a summer course in blacksmithing. One Sunday afternoon I drove him back to the campsite where the course was held and he showed me around, explaining about the process he used to purify and shape the metal he was sculpting. My friend took the class to learn more about sculpting with metal, but during our tour, he taught me a valuable lesson about how attentive God is to us.

My friend showed me the blacksmith shop where he worked on his class projects. It was a very hot July day, and I commented that it must be very sweltering work. He indicated that it indeed was very uncomfortable, but that he had to sit patiently, holding the metal in the hottest part of the flames. This was necessary, he explained, in order to burn off the impurities in the metal. Otherwise, it might break under the strain of shaping it on the anvil. Even though sweat would pour down his face and neck, soaking the heavy shirt he had to wear under his leather shop apron for protection, he could not take his eyes off of the metal in the fire for even an instant. He had to remain vigilant because if the metal were to be left in the flames for even a moment too long, it might be damaged beyond repair.

On the drive home, I found myself pondering this process. I began to realize that it could be seen as a metaphor for God's attentive action in our lives. I suppose that when we are experiencing some difficult challenge in our lives, it is easy to blame God for letting us suffer or for abandoning us when we seem to need Him the most. Lots of people seem to give in to that temptation. But as I drove back over the mountains to the Archabbey that afternoon, it occurred to me that maybe God is like a blacksmith or a goldsmith or a silversmith.

They say that a silversmith can tell when the silver is fully refined when he can see his image in it. Maybe that is what our struggles do for us. The prophet Malachi long, long ago used this same metaphor to comfort the people of Israel when they thought God had abandoned them to their troubles. He reassured them of God's presence among them saying:

> ... he is like the refiner's fire
> or like the fuller's lye.
> He will sit refining and purifying [silver],
> and he will purify the sons of Levi,
> Refining them like gold or like silver .... (Malachi 3:2-3).

If God is like a silversmith or a blacksmith, and I am convinced that He is, that means that He never takes His eyes off of us when we find ourselves in a hot spot. It means that the problem or crisis we find so burdensome has the potential to burn away our impurities, leaving us shining and beautiful.

As I thought about what my friend had explained about smithing, I realized that it is an apt metaphor for reminding us that suffering can have meaning and purpose in our lives, not as punishment, but rather, purification, in order that we might more fully reflect the image and likeness of God. The next time you're feeling like things are heating up in your life, have courage! Remember that God has His eye on you and will never look away until He sees His image and likeness shining in you.

# BEAUTIFUL MISTAKES

Like most gardeners, I have one spot in my garden that is a genuine annoyance to me. It is a corner of my garden that gets practically no sunlight and where nothing I have attempted to grow has been successful. After several years of sinking money into various attempts to cultivate some plant that would lend the corner a modicum of aesthetic dignity, I gave up. It became the site in my garden where my storage shed and potting bench are located. There was nothing else I could think of to do with that corner except make it a work space since it was barren. Fortunately, this desolate corner is relatively out of the view of most onlookers, but it still aggravates me.

One year I became so frustrated that when a large bag of potting soil burst, I just left it in a mound on the ground next to the potting bench. I did not even bother to clean it up or spread it around. I just left it and used another bag of soil to finish potting up seeds. The days lengthened and grew warmer, and spring blossomed into summer. All over the garden annuals and perennials exploded into a riot of color. The only dull spot was the mound of spilt potting soil. Gradually summer faded into autumn. I went about the usual depressing chore of cleaning up the garden for winter and packing away the tools in the shed and the empty seed flats in the potting bench for the next season. I noticed the mound of dirt next to the potting bench, but in my irritation, ignored it. It was as black and barren that November as it had been when the bag burst the preceding April. Not even weeds had grown on it.

The mound was still there when the spring thaw finally came the next year, still bleak, still barren. Not even the melting snow and spring rains had eroded it. In my eagerness to get the garden started, I attempted to pot up seed flats one breezy day in April, but soon gave up in frustration as the potting soil kept blowing and scattering the impatiens seeds I was trying to plant. I decided to try again on a calmer day.

As the gardening season progressed, and spring became summer, I paid no attention to the corner by the potting bench. My work there had long since ended. But when I returned from my vacation one beautiful July day to check on my garden, and went to the shed in search of hose and watering can, I found an amazing surprise. The mound of spilt potting soil was now a vibrant cascade of impatiens in red and white and rose! I stood mesmerized at the now blossoming corner, wondering how this had come to be. I can only deduce that before I gave up planting seeds on that blustery April day, the wind had borne some of the impatiens seeds onto the useless mound of potting soil that had stood barren for so long. I had tried planting impatiens there before, but they had never survived because the ground was chronically wet in that corner. Where not even ferns would grow before, I surmised that the pile of spilt potting soil had remedied the excess moisture problem. A solution that had never occurred to me had been wrought by my mistake and frustration.

Like that troublesome corner in my garden, we each bear our own unique flaws, wounds and imperfections. Maybe when we're having a bad day, we tend to focus on these flaws and how they prevent us from accomplishing all the good we want to bring about. Perhaps when we're having a bad day, we fail to recognize that God can use even our flaws in His time, in His way, according to His plan to work the good in us and for others that He needs us to do.

Evangelist and writer Patsy Clairmont often uses the metaphor of the cracked pot to explain how God works even through our imperfections. She writes of a vision in which she saw God scoop up a handful of light and place it in a pot with cracks in its sides, asking her to describe what she saw. Mrs. Clairmont tells of how the light shone out through the cracks and how the Lord explained that such was His love and His grace working through our imperfections.

I guess that is the lesson the barren corner of my garden taught me. When I tried to do all the right things on my own, nothing worked. But when I made a couple of mistakes: wasting an entire bag of soil in my carelessness and wasting seed in my rush to create beauty before its proper season, God transformed that ugly mud hole into a thing of beauty in spite of my impatience and frustration.

We don't need to be afraid of our imperfections, but we do need to honestly acknowledge them. Only then, can we, too, be instruments of God's grace. As the Lord told Saint Paul, *my grace is sufficient for you, for power is made perfect in weakness* (2Cor 12:9).

# GOD DOES NOT TURN AWAY

As I write this it has been a year since the fateful September morning in 2001 when our nation was the victim of terrorism. This has been a very difficult year for Americans as we tried to heal and recover, not only from the physical injuries visited upon us on the morning of September 11th, 2001, but also from the emotional wounds we sustained on that dreadful day. A great many of us, who were born after World War II, had never known, and indeed could not even begin to fathom, a day when our home soil would be brutally attacked in a savage act of aggression. Perhaps the greatest shock for many of us was to recognize our own vulnerability.

What we have seen in the past year is a tremendous response to that tragedy and a momentous growth in the American spirit, a change that has spawned countless acts of heroism not only in response to the attack of 911, but to all manner of challenges throughout the past year. We have seen America at its finest.

We have also witnessed Americans coming together to pray in a solidarity that many of us have never witnessed before. It has truly been a beautiful year in that regard. For a time after

September 11th, I noticed a dramatic increase in the number of persons attending Mass and seeking healing in the sacrament of Reconciliation. It has truly been a magnificent blessing to me to be called to minister during this special time in our nation's history.

As the months have gone by, the number of those participating at Mass and other religious services and sacraments has once again dropped back. I find this realization particularly disconcerting because the work of recovery is not finished. In fact, we have only begun to heal.

In a time and situation not so very different from our own, God promised the nation of Israel, *and if my people, upon whom my name has been pronounced, humble themselves and pray, and seek my presence. . . . I will heal them from heaven . . . and revive their lands.* (2 Chronicles 7:14).

Throughout the past year, we have seen in many and varied ways God working in our midst, fulfilling this very promise again and again. We cannot cease to humble ourselves before him and to pray. There will be many services and events in area churches and communities this week to remember the events of September 11th, 2001. Insofar as your schedule permits, try to join with others in prayer. We pray for those who were killed in the attacks. We pray for those they left behind and who mourn them. We pray for our service men and women, who at great personal sacrifice, are working to bring an end to terrorism for us and our children. We pray for each other. But perhaps most of all, let us not fail to utter a profound prayer of thanksgiving because, as a very wise and dear friend of mine once taught me, we can "be strengthened by the fact that the God who shares our joys, tastes the salt of our tears — and does not turn away from us."

# 5
# STEPPING STONES

*Therefore, brothers, stand firm and hold fast to the traditions that you were taught ...* (2Thes 2:15)

Kiskiminetas River, Armstrong County, Pennsylvania. Photo by Tom Metzgar.

# BUILDING BRIDGES

When I was a freshman at the University of Pittsburgh, I worked in the Admissions and Financial Aid Office. One day, I had to assemble information packets for new students. Among the materials was a poem called *The Bridge Builder,* by Will Allen Dromgoole. I kept a copy of that poem, and read and re-read it again and again because it resonated with something in my heart. As a young teacher, I claimed it as my philosophy of teaching, and later, it became an apt expression for the way I believe we are called as Christians to live in all aspects of our lives. In order to fully appreciate its message, I ask that you read it aloud — slowly and thoughtfully.

*An old man, going a lone highway,*
*Came at the evening, cold and gray,*
*To a chasm, vast and deep and wide,*
*Through which was flowing a sullen tide.*
*The old man crossed in the twilight dim*
*That sullen stream held no fears for him;*
*But he turned, when he reached the other side,*
*And built a bridge to span the tide.*

*"Old man," said a fellow pilgrim near,*
*"You are wasting your strength in building here.*

*Your journey will end with the ending day;*
*You never again must pass this way.*
*You have crossed the chasm deep and wide,*
*Why build you the bridge at the eventide?"*

*The builder lifted his old gray head,*
*"Good friend, in the path that I have come," he said,*
*"There followeth after me today,*
*A youth whose feet must pass this way.*
*This chasm which has been nought to me,*
*To that fair-headed youth may a pitfall be.*
*He, too, must cross in the twilight dim;*
*Good friend, I am building the bridge for him."*

I gave a framed copy of this poem to my father when he retired after 31 years as a high school teacher and principal. That was the year I entered the monastery. I was 30 years old. For me, Dad is the old man in the poem. I have known him in my lifetime to be a bridge builder in all things. Because Dad's words and example taught me the importance of building bridges, I became a teacher and administrator like him, and ultimately, a monk and priest.

Reflect on your life. Who has built bridges for you? Whether they be living or deceased, thank your bridge builders in some way. Secondly, seek out a bridge builder. In the book of Sirach we read:

*Reject not the tradition of old men*
*which they have learned from their fathers;*
*From it you will obtain the knowledge*
*how to answer in time of need* (Sir 8:9).

Lastly, take steps to build a bridge for someone in your life.

# GRATEFUL MOURNING

*The curfew tolls the knell of parting day,*
*The lowing herd wind slowly o'er the lea,*
*The plowman homeward plods his weary way,*
*And leaves the world to darkness and to me.*

*Now fades the glimmering landscape on the sight,*
*And all the air a solemn stillness holds ...*

Thomas Gray's *Elegy Written in a Country Churchyard* pays tribute to the ancestors of his village. I am often reminded of Gray's sentiments as autumn eases toward winter. The days grow shorter and the glorious reds and golds of autumn wane to somber brown; the bright, sunny days become cold and gray, and I recall that just as Nature has its cycle of living and dying, our lives do too. It is just as Ecclesiastes says there is:

*A time to be born, and a time to die;*

*a time to plant, and a time to uproot the plant* (3:2).

Is this a time for sadness? I feel sad sometimes at this time of year because I long for my family and friends who have died and my heart breaks under the weight of thoughts about what

139

I would, should or could have said or done. But when I begin to feel sad or lonely, I remember that I am not cut off from those I love. Just as we are united to them through our baptism into the Mystical Body of Christ, our union with our departed loved ones goes on. The Church celebrates the feast of All Saints on November 1. We celebrate all those who, having "run the race," have earned the crown of heaven. Through their merits and prayers, they assist us on our journey. They are spiritual bridge-builders for us. The following day, the feast of All Souls, is a special day set aside to pray for those who have reached the end of their earthly journey, but have not attained the joy of heaven. *All who die in God's grace and friendship, but still imperfectly purified, are indeed assured of their eternal salvation; but after death they undergo purification [Purgatory], so as to achieve the holiness necessary to enter the joy of heaven* (Catechism, 1030). We know that our prayers can help our loved ones because Scripture teaches us, *he made atonement for the dead that they might be freed from this sin* (2Macc 12:46).

Make time to pray for your loved ones who have died. Give thanks for their presence in your life, and ask God's mercy on all the souls in Purgatory. It's an opportunity not only to pray for the faithful departed, but to comfort those who mourn among us.

# BEDROCK

One year, when we celebrated the Holy Family, I had the privilege of celebrating the feast at home, with my own family. I was home for some days of rest and to be nurtured with my sisters at my parents' hearth and hearts.

I am not sure what makes some families work better than others — why some families manage to stay close and others barely speak. I have pondered this question long and hard, and if I have no clear answers, I do have some theories.

It seems to me that one reason why my family stayed close is because the importance of family was taught to us as early as we could understand. We were taught that family was the center, the root, around which our lives revolved. Maybe we were taught this because my father learned it from his immigrant parents. This notion of being centered in the family suggests a stance toward life that says that life isn't about me — that my individual wants or needs are not the most important thing — that my existence is not singular — but rather, that my life takes its meaning from a context — the kinship or clan ties that keep me anchored to that root.

Another reason why my family has stayed close is because

there was sacred time — time we spent together specifically as family. Dinnertime was one such time. Every night at 5:00 we sat down to dinner — all of us. It was understood that our friends did not call during the dinner hour. Nor was the television or radio on while we ate. Dinnertime was about being together, about appreciating each other, and it never began without Dad's praying the "grace."

*Bless us, O Lord,*
*And these thy gifts,*
*Which we are about to receive,*
*From thy bounty*
*Through Christ, our Lord.*
*May God provide for the wants of others,*
*And may the souls of the faithful departed,*
*Through the mercy of God,*
*Rest in peace. Amen.*

That simple prayer taught us to ask God's blessing on ourselves, to recognize the food as gift, to recognize the role of Christ as mediator, to pray for the wants of others, and to pray for the faithful departed. Less than one minute of each day spent in that common prayer, yet so much faith transmitted.

We went to church as a family. If there were one single thing I could fix about Christian life as it is lived today, this would be it: I would insist that families worship together — not in shifts, not just those who feel like going that day — but every member, together.

The fact is family life is the cornerstone of any culture. Sociology teaches us that culture is acquired— it is learned through the active transmission of that culture from one generation to the next. But we have stopped transmitting the Christian family culture that we were given. Why?

Isaiah reminds us:

*Look to the rock from which you were hewn,*
    *to the pit from which you were quarried;*
*Look to Abraham, your father,*
    *and to Sarah, who gave you birth.* (Is 51:1-2).

Consider your family life. Is there anything in it that needs changing? Resolve to spend more quality time together.

# PUMPKINS WITH PAP

One January day, I noticed that it was still daylight when I got home from work. As spring approaches, there are things that gardeners can be doing to prepare. According to one garden calendar, January is the time for planning our garden, ordering seed catalogues, servicing our garden power equipment and ordering fertilizer.

When the winter has grown long and wearying, I enjoy looking at gardening books and imagining what my garden might look like. I love the beautiful plants and bright colors in the photos, and with a steaming cup of herbal tea and a throw tossed over my lap as I sit in my rocking chair, I can create some rare, quiet moments of blissful peace, even if the wind is howling just outside my window.

I have a small porch next to my monastery room. Each year, I plant window boxes to soften its austere cement walls and to add a splash of color to the drab, gray concrete. I remember a time when I did have a garden. I remember a time when I grew pumpkins, and what I learned.

I was about eleven, and Dad had started a small garden that

we were sharing with a neighbor. I planted pumpkin seeds. I was so excited when they began to sprout! I rushed off the school bus every afternoon to see how much they'd grown. However, it had only been a couple of weeks when we determined that the pumpkins had to go — the little garden didn't have enough room for them. But my Grandfather had a bigger garden. So Mom and I dug up the pumpkins one morning, wrapped them in wet newspaper to protect them, and drove off to Grandma and Grandpap's house. Grandpap had already prepared the soil for them and so we carefully planted them. Then Mom took me home. It was a good thing. Apparently, pumpkin vines do not take to transplanting. They were a wilted, drooping mess. But Grandpap kept after them, watering them a couple times a day — which was a sacrifice since he and Grandma had a well, not city water. By the time I got back to Grandma and Grandpap's house the following weekend, it was evident there had been a mortal struggle in the pumpkin patch, but there was also new growth — a sign that the vines would survive and bear fruit. That summer, I got to know Grandpap in a special, "just him and me" kind of way. We watched the pumpkins begin to form on the vines and grow bigger and bigger until they started to darken to orange.

That was probably the best summer of my boyhood. I wish every kid could get to grow pumpkins. It's not just about the science you learn by growing them, it's about truly priceless moments you spend with Grandpap. It's about the wind and the rain and the sun. It's about the bright colors and the earthy smells and being close to creation. It's about being in the presence of someone who is wise. It's about seeing the face of God in Grandpap's face. It's about that rare smile that makes you know he loves you in a special way, even if he has twenty other grandchildren.

Think about your garden — your spiritual one. What virtue do you plan to grow? *Make no mistake: God is not mocked. For a person will reap only what he sows. For in due time we shall reap our harvest, if we do not give up.* (Gal 6:7, 9).

# FAITH-FILLED PHRASES

The other day my good friend, Father Jim, from Our Lady of Victory Maronite Catholic Church called me. Without even thinking, I greeted him in the traditional Lebanese way. When he asked me in return, "Keefek Aboona," or "How are you, Father?" I heard the Lebanese response fall from my lips, "Nish-kor Allah, ham-dil-la." It basically translates in English as "I thank God because He is deserving of my thanks," but among the Lebanese people this expression is used in the same way as we use "fine, thanks."

It was the unconscious way in which the Arabic response came to me that got me to thinking about our ethnic customs and what they say about how we view the world. I think that it is the idioms and expressions we use automatically more than any grandiose statements we may profess that really reveal our world view.

Until I was eight years old, we lived only two doors down from my father's sister and his mother. Just from the sheer proximity, my sisters and I were exposed to our Lebanese culture more during those early years than to my mother's German-Irish heritage. That exposure shaped us and our view of the world for the rest of our lives.

To make the response that "I thank God because He is deserving of my thanks," communicates much, much more about me than the simple fact that "I am doing just fine." It says in a clear way that I attribute my being "fine" to God's generous care for me. It says a lot about how I see the world, and more than that, it catechizes those who hear me.

There are a lot of other examples that I can think of from when I was a child. For example, we would frequently hear the exclamation, "y' Allah," meaning "God be praised" or "Oh my God!"

How often when she was exasperated with us would Mom warn us with "God help you!" and as a prayer against some impending harm or bad situation, "God forbid!"

We never left my aunt's house without hearing from my Uncle Bill, "God go with you, habeebee," meaning honey, and when we'd call back "See you soon," we never heard simply, "OK" or "I'll look forward to it," but always, always came the response, "God willing."

Today my sisters and I are grown and their children are growing fast. But you would still hear these same expressions in our households. Unfortunately, we have been shaped by the modern culture as well, and so you wouldn't hear these old sayings as much as we did when we were children. Contemporary expressions are used now. But the idioms society uses today do not make mention of, or call upon, God. And I think that is very regrettable, for I am afraid that it means that we Christians are not as aware of God's presence in the ordinariness of our daily life together as we should be.

My whole life, my vocation as a monk and my vocation as a

priest were shaped by my parents', grandparents' and aunts' and uncles' sincere belief in God's presence and intervention in every aspect of life, no matter how small. They taught me and my sisters that same faith by these little sayings. If this generation is not using the same expressions, I find myself sadly pondering two questions: Does that mean we no longer believe in God's Providence in our lives? And how will we transmit that basic faith in Divine Providence to our children?

Give some thought to the sayings you grew up hearing and how they have affected your view of the world. Every ethnicity has its treasury of expressions. Consider how much or how little you use them today. Why or why not? Maybe if we bring back some of these idioms into our everyday usage, we'll find a subtle change in our faith life as well.

*When I was my father's child,*
*frail, yet the darling of my mother,*
*He taught me, and said to me:*
*"Let your heart hold fast my words:*
*keep my commands, that you may live!*
*"Get wisdom, get understanding!*
*Do not forget or turn aside from the*
*words I utter." (Prov 4:3-5).*

Do not underestimate the importance of our ethnic expressions in transmitting the faith. Meanwhile, "Allah ma'ak,""God go with you!"

# LOVING-KINDNESS

When we enter the season of Lent, it is important to stop and reflect on issues that really matter. On Ash Wednesday, the prophet Joel calls to us to enter fully into the spirit of repentance that will prepare us to celebrate the greatest of all feasts — Easter, the feast of the Resurrection. Is not life — eternal life — the greatest of all God's gifts to us? It is this most precious gift that we prepare to celebrate during the season of Lent. Lent takes on a penitential character as we recognize that we have not responded to God's gifts with the wholehearted love that He deserves. Each day of Lent offers us a fresh opportunity to make that love response.

*Even now, says the LORD,*
> *return to me with your whole heart,*
> *with fasting and weeping, and mourning* (Joel 2:12).

What is it that we should mourn? For what ought we to weep? It seems to me that we would do well to weep and mourn for the missed opportunities to love others as freely and generously as God has loved us. And while we have the practice of making sacrifices during Lent, Isaiah reminds us that those sacrifices must not be halfhearted:

*[Share] your bread with the hungry,*
   *[shelter] the oppressed and the homeless;*
 *[Clothe] the naked when you see them,*
    *and [do not turn] your back on your own* (Is 58:7)

So often, when we think about people in need, we think of the most obvious examples that Isaiah listed. Indeed, such individuals are worthy of our care and concern. But perhaps we also need to be mindful of other ways that we might be turning our backs on our own. How often do we fail to offer a word of encouragement or a warm smile to a co-worker we pass in the hall or encounter at the photocopy machine? How often do we only half-listen to someone at home when he is sharing a concern or telling of a small daily triumph? How frequently do we focus on the little ways in which our family members annoy us instead of looking at the larger picture of their love for us? How quick are we to snap at someone for a minor infraction, just because we feel pressured about something completely unrelated? How often do we choose to cling to petty grudges when we could easily forgive and forget?

In the Hebrew Scriptures, much is said about God's *hesed* for us. This ancient Hebrew word translates into English as the concept of loving-kindness. Another way of looking at the questions above might be to consider our response to the loving-kindness that people all around us show us each day. Jesus insisted that his disciples fulfill two components of the Law of Moses: *You shall love the LORD, your God, with all your heart, and with all your soul, and with all your strength* (Deut 6:5) and secondly, *You shall love your neighbor as yourself* (Lev 19:18). We are obliged to love God so wholeheartedly because He has first loved us, showering his loving-kindness upon us in countless ways. We must love our neighbor for two reasons. First, when we love our neighbor, we honor the image and likeness of the Creator, in which, Genesis teaches us, all human beings are made. Secondly, we best show ourselves to be made in God's image and likeness when we imitate Him by sharing the loving-kindness we have so freely received from His hand.

Sometimes the people who are the hungry, oppressed and homeless that Isaiah talks about are those who are right under our noses. They are the very same people who make us feel special and human, who have touched our lives in simple but profound ways. Wouldn't a beautiful way to observe Lent be to repent of the many ways in which we have ignored God's choicest gifts to us, to turn back to Him and to thank Him for the people who have touched us? Perhaps we might send a note or card to even one person who comes to mind as we reflect on that question, letting him or her know that we appreciate the impact that he or she has made in our lives. What would the sacrifice amount to? Maybe five or ten minutes of our time? But what a difference it would make to those who have taken far more time to care about us. Wouldn't that be a wonderful way to reflect on a different one of the questions above?

If we were to do this, wouldn't the words of Isaiah ring true in our lives:

*... then your light shall break forth like the dawn,*
*and your wound shall quickly be healed;*
*Your vindication shall go before you,*
*and the glory of the LORD shall be your rear guard* (Is 58:8).

We would then truly be the salt of the earth and the light of the world.

# WISDOM COMES WITH AGE

When I was growing up, one of my favorite television programs was *The Waltons*. In my house, we loved that show, partly because it was good entertainment, but also because my mother had grown up in a situation not all that different from that of the family portrayed in the program. Both of my parents grew up during the Great Depression, but my father grew up in a town. My mother, on the other hand, could easily identify with the characters on the show and the stories they portrayed. She had grown up in a more rural setting, her home surrounded by those of her uncles and cousins. Watching the show with Mom was like attending a very exciting history class because she would share vignettes from her own girlhood that fascinated and captivated my sisters and me. It made the show much more real for us, and taught us a lot about who we are. As I look back on the many lessons that The Waltons offered American television viewers, I suppose that one thing that strikes me now is the way in which they cared for their elderly. Grandma and Grandpa Walton were an integral part of the household and figured prominently in the lives of the children.

American society has changed a great deal from the time of

the Great Depression, and it is much less common that three generations of a family share one house. In this day, it is more often necessary that the elderly live in nursing homes or assisted living arrangements.

When I was assigned to a parish, I often found myself visiting parishioners that lived in nursing homes or skilled care facilities. It was one of the most enjoyable aspects of my work, far easier for me than hospital ministry. But in a way, it was also more sad. I could often tell, without even asking the nursing staff, which residents had received visits from their families and which were lonely. There seemed to be a distinct difference in their demeanors.

Mother Teresa of Calcutta commented on this topic when she addressed the National Prayer Breakfast in 1994, the Year of the Family. Mother Teresa noted, *I can never forget the experience that I had in visiting a home where they kept all these old parents of sons and daughters who had just put them into an institution and forgotten them – maybe. I saw that in the home these old people had everything – good food, comfortable place, television, everything, but everyone was looking toward the door. And I did not see a single one with a smile on the face. I turned to Sister and I asked: "Why do these people who have every comfort here, why are they all looking toward the door? Why are they not smiling?*

*I am so used to seeing the smiles on our people, even the dying ones smile. And Sister said: "This is the way it is nearly every day. They are expecting, they are hoping that a son or daughter will come to visit them. They are hurt because they are forgotten." And see, this neglect to love brings spiritual poverty. Maybe in our own family we have somebody who is feeling lonely, who is feeling sick, who is feeling worried. Are we there? Are we willing to give until it hurts in order to be with our families, or do we put our own interests first? These are questions we must ask ourselves, especially as we begin this year of the family. We must remember that love begins at home and we must also remember that "the future of humanity passes through the family."*

Mother Teresa used very strong language in her address, but as I reflected on her words, I was reminded of two powerful lessons. The first has to do with respecting our elders. All throughout the scriptures, we are reminded again and again of the importance of respecting and caring for the aged. *Stand up in the presence of the aged, and show respect for the old* (Lev 19:32). Wisdom comes with age, and long life was seen to be the reward for goodness. Therefore, the young were expected to revere the old. On those who chose not to show respect to their seniors, Divine retribution was anticipated.

*The eye that mocks a father,*
*or scorns an aged mother,*
*Will be plucked out by the ravens in the valley;*
*the young eagles will devour it* (Prov 30:17).

I am sure that most of us do the very best that we can by our parents and grandparents. I have watched many people struggle with decisions about eldercare. Such choices are never made easily, and those who find themselves confronted with such decisions deserve our prayerful support. The second moral that I thought about is about the importance of being mindful of the messages and lessons that we unwittingly transmit to our children when they observe us interacting with our seniors. More than what any authority figure might say or teach, children are most influenced by what their parents and significant others do and say. Research in psychology has reinforced this notion repeatedly. So think carefully about what your actions, attitudes, facial expressions, gestures and words teach the youngsters around you. If Mother Teresa was correct in the assertion that *the future of humanity passes through the family,* and I believe that she absolutely was, then we need to be vigilant about the model that we provide to our children.

# LIFE 101

I recall the first event of my college orientation as if it were yesterday. It was a hot August afternoon. We were herded into a large auditorium, several hundred of us freshman, yet a mere fraction of the class of 1984. I remember feeling utterly lost in a sea of humanity. It took some time for the crowd to quiet, but when we had, the dean approached the microphone. He told us to look at the person on our left. Then he said to look at the person on our right. After a pregnant pause, owing largely to our confusion about why we were being told to look at people, the dean continued, "In four years, neither of the people you looked at will still be here." Then he launched into a speech about how difficult college was and how much we needed to study, the kind of canned speech that I imagine every dean on every college campus in America was making that weekend. It did not inspire confidence.

Such was my orientation to college life. It was not the warmest welcome, but I came to learn that there was a kernel of truth in what the dean had said that day. Many of my friends and acquaintances came and went during the years that I studied at the university; some because they chose to be distracted by the glamour of college life at its wildest, some through no fault of their own, but the warp and weft of the class of 1984 definitely changed, just like the dean had foretold.

I recall that as I looked to my left that first afternoon, I noticed an elderly woman sitting several seats down the row from me. I remember thinking at the time that somebody's grandmother must have insisted on attending the opening assembly, no doubt to the great embarrassment of her grandson or granddaughter. But a few days later, while I stood outside the Biology building talking with an acquaintance, Andy, I saw the same woman slowly making her way across Fifth Avenue toward where we stood talking, waiting for class to begin. The woman stopped in front of the Biology building, pulled a paper out of her bag, studied it briefly, looked up to read the sign outside the building, and then began to make her way slowly up the steps toward Andy and me. Several of the students gathered in groups along the wide steps that led up to the building's entrance paused long enough to smirk at the old woman before retreating into huddles from which laughter erupted in the poor woman's wake. Even Andy and I paused in our conversation long enough to ponder what the old woman was doing there. She seemed too old to be the professor.

We surmised rightly that the woman was not the professor. Much to my utter surprise, I came to learn that the woman was a student like me. Along with about six hundred other students, she was enrolled in the same section of Biology 11 as Andy and I.

Over the course of my first semester at the university, I came to learn many lessons about the elderly. I grew in my respect of my seniors by way of the poise and dignity this woman brought to our class. Gradually, I came to appreciate the quiet courage that made it possible for her to undertake learning at a time in life when memorization does not come especially easily. I slowly began to realize that life is not over when we reach retirement age, but rather when we stop learning about our world, because each new day unfolds another aspect of the mystery of life if we choose to be attentive to it. I came to understand that true wisdom comes not from book learning when we are young, but rather from a stance of openness in the face of new challenges even when we could choose to pass them by. I came to believe that taking risks, even hard risks, keeps us vital, while choosing the safer route of comfortable acquiescence ultimately shrivels us. I learned that growing older is not about being confined to home. Life continues to be about sharing our gifts and talents, even if we have to move a little more slowly to do so. I learned that the only thing that limits my dreams is fear, and fear is foolish. I also learned that I had a lot more to learn.

Fortunately, I have been blessed with the opportunity to continue to study under the tutelage of wise elders. I have received a tremendous gift in working with the many generous seniors who volunteer their time in the varied ministries of the Parish, the Basilica Gift Shop and the Gristmill General Store at Saint Vincent Archabbey. It would be accurate to say that my sense of what it means to mature has been radically changed by their presence in my life. I certainly have grown through their ministry to me. They have laid stepping stones for me to follow. Give some thought to your relationship with the seniors in your life. When is the last time you had a conversation with one of them and allowed yourself to gain some wisdom? Take a few minutes out of your busy schedule and sit down with a cup of tea and one of your elders. If you allow yourself to listen, you might just learn the lesson of a lifetime.

*The teaching of the wise is a fountain of life,*
*that a man may avoid the snares of death* (Prov 13:14).

# TABLE TREASURES

Back in the days before I came to the monastery, when I thought that I would marry and have a family and a home of my own, my sisters and I would occasionally find ourselves caught up in banter about which of my parents' belongings each of us wanted to inherit some day long, long hence. My sisters were mainly interested in my mother's jewelry and china. The only thing I wanted in the whole house was my parents' dining room set.

Our dining room set is antique. It had belonged to my Grandmother Kanfush, but my parents got it as a cast-off when Grandma got a new dining room set after what we refer to as "the fire." The fire happened in 1956. January 30, 1956. The reason I know this is that "the fire" has been etched into our family folklore and our collective memory, even though it happened before all but my sisters Denise and Ladonna were born.

Ladonna's christening was on January 29th. My parents were staying at my Grandmother's home because my father had just gotten out of the Air Force. In the afternoon on the day after the christening, the furnace exploded. The furnace was located in the basement directly under the dining room in my

Grandmother's house. The floor, not surprisingly, began to cave in from the flames, drawing the dining room set and my sister Ladonna in her bassinet along with it. Fortunately, Grandma's quick action saved Ladonna, but it was too late for the dining set. My parents lost everything but the clothes on their backs and the mustering-out pay that my mother ran back into the burning house to salvage from their bedroom closet once my two sisters were safe.

The dining room set was irreparably damaged. In the fire, the buffet and two or three chairs were lost entirely; the table was damaged but salvageable, along with the china cabinet and server. It was these pieces along with the remaining chairs that became my parents' first and only "good" dining room set, damaged and incomplete as they are. Back in 1972, not quite a year after we moved into our new house, while we were at our church hall celebrating my sister Denise's graduation from high school, the table was damaged again when some of my father's high school students took a garden pick and pitched it through the sliding glass doors, embedding it in the table top to get back at my father for some discipline he had imposed on them for breaking school rules. For a time after that incident, the table had to be in a shop to be repaired, but other than that, it has been the one piece of furniture in my parents' home that has never been updated or replaced. For most of my life, my parents wouldn't have been able to afford to replace the old dining set with a new one because there were just too many mouths to feed and extra money was scarce. As we kids got older and times got better, they could have gotten something newer, but I'm awfully glad they never did.

So, why would I have wanted the damaged goods for my

own home? It's simple — for the history.

That table is where every holiday meal of my home life took place. It is at that table that we kids learned our story: what it means to be a Kanfush, to be Lebanese and what it means to be a Farland and German-Irish. At that table we heard the stories of our ancestors who traveled from Lebanon to break bread at that very table and of the Great Flood in Johnstown which brought the Farlands to Beaver County.

We were taught the lessons of our religion by way of the blessings and prayers my father made it his custom to offer before each and every holiday meal. We were taught the importance of serving others through our service at that table. Though it is now rare for me to be at the table for meals, I still gravitate to my place which was nearest the kitchen that as the youngest, I might help my mother to clear dishes and to serve throughout the meal.

That same table saw the joy of as many Christmases and Easters as I can remember. Our graduations, Confirmations, First Communions and weddings were all celebrated about that table. It has functioned as the buffet table from which our guests have been served for our christenings, as well as the christenings of our children. It is also where we shared our sadness and grief when our family circle diminished. It provided the meal when my nieces Christy and Emily were baptized together as cousins on the very same day that we gathered at the funeral home for my Grandmother Farland's wake, just two weeks before my sister Aileen got married. That table has seen it all. If only it could tell the story.

My parents' dining room table is my family history. There we have given and received unconditional love and there we have battled as if to the death for philosophical points that hardly seem relevant now. But always, *always,* we gathered there as family — in love.

Think about your family. Do you eat together? Are you building memories for your children to cherish? Are you teaching them the stories that tell them who they are? If not, start. Start right now, before it's too late. And may the blessing of the psalmist be yours:

*Like olive plants*
  *your children around your table* (Ps 128:3).

# FREE TO DREAM

*When in the course of human events, it becomes necessary for one people to dissolve the political bands which have connected them with another, and to assume among the powers of the earth the separate and equal station to which the Laws of Nature and of Nature's God entitle them, a decent respect to the opinions of mankind requires that they should declare the causes which impel them to the separation.*

*We hold these truths to be self-evident, that all men are created equal, that they are endowed by their Creator with certain unalienable Rights, that among these are Life, Liberty and the pursuit of Happiness.*

So begins the Declaration of Independence, issued as a unanimous declaration of the thirteen United States of America on July 4, 1776. We proudly celebrate it every year. Yet, at the same time, we must acknowledge that our history has been checkered with contradictions to this declaration. We cannot help but remember a day, December 1, 1955, when Mrs. Rosa Parks was arrested for refusing to give up a seat in the last row of seats reserved for white people on a bus in Montgomery, Alabama, sparking the Civil Rights movement nearly one hundred years after African-Americans were freed from the tyranny of slavery. We did not practice segregation here in the North, and African-Americans were not prevented from voting here as they were in the deep south as recently as August 28, 1963, when Dr. Martin Luther King Jr. delivered his famous address on the steps of the Lincoln Memorial in Washington, D.C. Dr. King proclaimed on that balmy afternoon, that he had a dream for our nation. His dream was that we would, in fact, operationalize our forefathers' belief that all men are created equal.

I was only 11 months old when Dr. King delivered his address — mercifully too young to have been aware of a time when segregation and racial prejudice split this land. Yet I am not too young to remember the regrettable day in January 1973, when the highest court in this land issued an opinion in the landmark case *Roe v. Wade* making legal abortion upon demand.

I was almost 11 years old on that occasion. But even then, it seemed to me that even though the esteemed justices found laws banning abortion to be in violation of the 14th amendment of our Constitution, the ruling somehow seemed to contradict the notion that all men have an unalienable right to life, liberty and the pursuit of happiness.

The dream that Martin Luther King Jr. proclaimed was not so far-fetched. It was the same dream that the prophet Isaiah envisioned when he spoke of freedom for the Israelite nation, divided, deported and exiled from its homeland in slavery and oppression under Nebuchadnezzar. Like Martin Luther King would do 2000 years later, Isaiah shared his vision to rally his people and to give them hope. But God's promise extends beyond the unique possession of any one race or nation.

*It is too little,* He tells Isaiah(Is 49:6),

165

*for you to be my servant,*
*to raise up the tribes of Jacob,*
*and restore the survivors of Israel;*
*I will make you a light to the nations,*
*that my salvation may reach to the ends of the earth.*

Some 550 years after Isaiah, John the Baptist also promised the people of his day hope, pointing to the freedom promised in the person of Jesus the Christ, the Lamb of God, who would free the whole world, taking away their sins and sending the Holy Spirit upon them. Isaiah's dream is fulfilled in Christ Jesus. We have received His Spirit and are called to continue His mission. And yet, the iniquity of abortion, which makes a mockery of our own Declaration of Independence continues. The United States cannot claim to champion democracy and equality to the rest of the world when we deny the fundamental rights and freedom we want others to espouse to the weakest members of our own society; not so long as we hold the unborn in chains of slavery — giving them no right to live, no voice to be heard. We fail in our mission to be a light to the nations, and the world recognizes this sad fact. As far away as India, Mother Teresa of Calcutta called us to recognize this failing when she noted, *Any country that accepts abortion is not teaching its people to love, but to use any violence to get what they want. This is why the greatest destroyer of love and peace is abortion.* As Catholic Christians — as Americans — we cannot remain silent in the face of abortion, of discrimination, of injustice of any kind. Not when this nation has been built upon a commitment to life, to freedom. As long as we remain silent, we lie in the face of the very truths which we claim to be self-evident: *that all men are created equal, that they are endowed by their Creator with certain unalienable Rights, that among these are Life, Liberty and the pursuit of Happiness.*

My brothers and sisters, by our baptism and birth in this great nation, we share a dream. We share this dream with Isaiah, with John the Baptist, with Jesus Christ, with Rosa Parks and with Martin Luther King Jr. It is a dream in which all peoples are one in the unity of the human family with Christ as head: old and young, rich and poor, born and unborn. Only when our dream is realized will we truly be a light to the nations.

Let us reflect on our obligation as Christians and Americans to be a light to the nations, and let us join our prayers to those who march in Washington, D.C. every year that slavery, that iniquity, that tyranny will end in this country, and that all people, born and unborn, will know freedom and life in Jesus Christ.

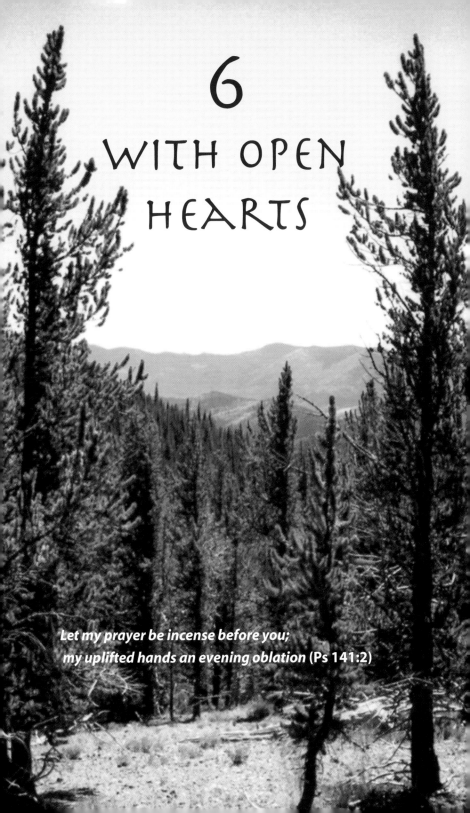

# 6
# WITH OPEN HEARTS

*Let my prayer be incense before you;*
*my uplifted hands an evening oblation (Ps 141:2)*

Continental Divide, Rocky Mountains, Colorado.
Photo by Kim Metzgar.

# PRAY WITHOUT CEASING

March means there really are signs of spring all around us. The snowdrops which grow in the lawns about the monastery begin to sprout. The same is true of the crocus planted in Father Sebastian's garden. When I am able to be outdoors to see all these early signs of spring, my heart soars, and I can appreciate the words of Saint Thérèse of Lisieux who wrote: *for me, prayer means launching out of the heart toward God; a cry of grateful love from the crest of joy or the trough of despair; it is a vast, supernatural force that opens out my heart, and binds me close to Jesus.*

Prayer is integral to the life of the monk. It is, for him, as natural as breathing, and should be as constant. I remember as a novice monk reading *The Way of the Pilgrim* and learning about *The Jesus Prayer.* In that story, the pilgrim is seeking an answer to the problem of how to satisfy the admonition in the First Letter to the Thessalonians to *pray without ceasing* (1Thess 5:17). The answer comes in the form of *The Jesus Prayer.* There are several versions of this ancient Eastern prayer, but the one I personally use is *"Lord Jesus Christ, Son of the Living God, have mercy on me, a sinner."*

I use this prayer, based in Luke's gospel (Lk 18:13-14) and

prayed from the time of the early Church, to recollect myself any time I'm nervous or anxious or want to quiet my soul. I breathe in on the phrase, *"Lord Jesus Christ,"* that I might breathe in the living Word through whom the universe was created. I exhale on the words *"Son of the Living God."* I inhale on *"have mercy on me,"* that I might breathe in God's mercy, and exhale on the words, *"a sinner,"* that I might let go of my sinfulness with each breath. Done slowly and purposefully, it serves to release me from my slavery to thoughts and cares which draw my attention away from God, and allows me to enter His presence. There I can rest peacefully, as Saint Thérèse puts it, in the crest of joy, or pour out my heart's concerns, as it were, from the trough of despair, even without words.

This is an example of what is known as apophatic prayer, an Eastern Christian method noted for a lack of images. In apophatic prayer, the goal is to empty one's consciousness of all thoughts, thereby entering into God's presence by means of an interior silence. This seems somewhat remote to the Western Christian mind, and directly contrasts with the kataphatic methods with which we are so familiar. In kataphatic prayer, mental images are important for focusing one's attention on God. The clearest example of kataphatic prayer is the practice of meditating on the mysteries of the Rosary, wherein we imagine the scenes of the Gospel while we pray the *Hail Marys*. Take some moments to review how you pray.

Try praying *The Jesus Prayer*. Settle yourself, and recite the prayer taking long, deep breaths. Give it just five minutes a day to see how it works for you. Perhaps you will find a moment of calm and peace wherein the Lord can speak to your heart.

# PILGRIMAGE

*The Jesus Prayer* is a form of apophatic prayer common among Eastern Christians. By apophatic, we mean those forms of prayer in which the mind is emptied of thoughts and images. In contrast, we are more familiar with kataphatic prayer, which are those forms of prayer in which an image, either visual or mental, is used to focus our thoughts and direct our prayerful meditation. Since we gather to pray the *Stations of the Cross* each Friday during Lent, I thought we might look at the history of the *Stations* so that we might better understand this beautiful and traditional form of prayer.

The *Stations of the Cross* are a form of kataphatic prayer. When we pray the *Stations,* we focus on images, fourteen in all. Though in recent years, some have added a fifteenth station. Through drawing to mind the events of Christ's Passion and reflecting on those events, we enter more fully into union with Jesus. We become one with those about whom Luke writes *a large crowd of people followed him, including many women who mourned and lamented him* (Luke 23:27).

The *Stations of the Cross* evolved from a practice of pilgrimage in the late 4th century. Byzantine pilgrims apparently visited Calvary and the Lord's tomb, but later other sites associated with His Passion were added. Beginning during the 14th century, under the guidance of Franciscan friars, pilgrims followed the footsteps of Jesus on his way to Calvary. At various points along the way, particular scenes from the Passion narratives were remembered.

For those who could not travel to the Holy Land, the *Stations of the Cross* became a popular way to enter into the spirit of pilgrimage. By the 18th century, the fourteen *Stations* as we know them were established consistently among churches and communities. We owe the Franciscans a debt of gratitude for their work in promoting this form of prayer.

Take your place in the crowd that followed Jesus. Allow yourself to enter into the spirit of pilgrimage. That is, after all, the nature of Lent. It is a time of pilgrimage in our relationship with the Lord.

# SILENCE

One of the monastic virtues I most treasure is silence. Trappist monk Charles Cummings, in his book *Monastic Practices* points out that silence has always been the milieu in which the word of God has been heard most clearly and understood most completely. The modern monk lives out his vocation in the context of an ongoing struggle between the contemplative and active aspects of his life. In parish work, as in all of our apostolates, I find that in order to effectively serve, it is essential that I maintain a balance between availability to others and availability to God in solitude and silence.

One of the most important lessons of my novice year in the monastery was learning to be comfortable in an atmosphere of silence. It is a difficult discipline to learn, but it is often the most noticed aspect of monastic life when outsiders are admitted as guests to the monastery building. Visiting priests and religious-brothers frequently comment on how quiet it is. But external silence is only one part of the discipline of silence. The novice monk also learns to cultivate an interior silence — a calming of the senses, mind and spirit that permits him to rest in the presence of the Trinity in a wordless prayer of adoration.

For some, the experience of silence can be uncomfortable. After all, we live in a society where we are constantly bombarded with stimuli both visual and audible. Noise can be a sign that we are not alone. But we need to remember that silence was the primordial state. Henri Nouwen eloquently states in his work *The Way of the Heart:*

*Out of eternal silence, God spoke the Word, and through this Word created and recreated the world. In the beginning, God spoke the land, the sea, and the sky. God spoke the sun, the moon, and the stars. God spoke plants, birds, fish, animals wild and tame. Finally, God spoke man and woman. Then, in the fullness of time, God's Word, through whom all had been created, became flesh and gave power to all who believe to become the children of God. In all this, the Word of God does not break the silence of God, but rather unfolds the immeasurable richness of that silence.*

So must it be with us. In the "busyness" of our lives, we generate a good deal of noise, both external and interior. When we join in God's ongoing act of creation through our work and in our relationships, we must be careful to remain respectful of the inner space in which the Spirit inspires us — and that of those with whom we live and work.

How do we do this? The novice monk learns to cultivate interior silence by way of baby steps. First, he is taught to value external silence. Television is forbidden and radio is limited. He is reminded not to speak in the hallways of the monastery unless necessary and to close doors softly. Gradually he learns to appreciate the solace of his monastic cell. Little by little, he learns to use certain techniques to enter into a space of interior silence. For me, *The Jesus Prayer* became the best technique for gently turning down the volume of my senses. But I still find it necessary to create "solitude sites" in my life where I can find refuge. My rocking chair is one of these, my monastic cell is another, as is the little meditation garden that I have created. It has become an island of refuge to which I can slip away for some quiet moments alone with God when the office gets a little too hectic for me to keep my balance.

Spend some moments reflecting on Nouwen's words. Find a place in your life where you can cultivate exterior silence. Bit by bit, you will find that interior calm follows. Only then can you let God's healing grace wash over you. Try it! You'll find a sense of peace in your life and experience the meaning of the words, *Silence, all mankind, in the presence of the LORD! for he stirs forth from his holy dwelling* (Zec 2:17), in your life. Consider that the Lord is coming forth to spend time alone with you!

# BINDINGS

From east to west, people of all ethnicities celebrate Saint Patrick's Day. It is an integral part of our American tradition. We dress in green, gather for parades and flock to pubs to listen to Irish folk music while sipping ale of an emerald hue.

Until very recently, the exuberance which we associate with Saint Patrick's Day was an American phenomenon. In Ireland, the day was observed more quietly, with Mass in the morning and feasting in the afternoon. The Lenten prohibition against meat was often lifted for the day to allow for the banqueting, but that was about the extent of the hoopla. The Irish celebration was not nearly as exuberant as the American observance of the feast day. Even the pubs in Ireland were all closed on Saint Patrick's Day — it was a religious holiday.

But who was this Saint Patrick whom we so heartily recall each year on March 17th? The only documents existing today that we know Patrick wrote are his *Confession* and a *Letter to Coroticus,* written to an Irish warlord that Patrick was forced to excommunicate. As such, the *Letter* doesn't provide much in the way of biographical data on Patrick. However, his *Confession* is an autobiographical account of his call to convert the Irish. From this, we know that Patrick was born in Britain to Roman parents more than a millenium and a half ago. Apparently, his family was somewhat wealthy. In a raid on Britain by the Irish, Patrick was captured as a teenager and taken to Ireland where he worked as a slave tending sheep until he escaped some six years later. Returning to Britain, Patrick studied for the priesthood, was ordained and eventually returned to Ireland, where he served as a missionary, priest and ultimately bishop. Though it is doubtful that Patrick ever drove the snakes out of Ireland, of his devotion to the Trinity there can be no doubt.

Patrick's story seems far removed from our own, but it isn't really. He stands as an example of one who heard the specific task to which God was calling him and followed it, even in spite of obstacles. How often do we fail to discern God's call in our lives and turn back at the first inconvenience or hurdle we encounter, treating it as an insurmountable obstacle? Patrick shows us what can be accomplished through prayer and perseverance. We would do well to imitate his life and his prayer. Reflect on this hymn about Saint Patrick written by Cecil Frances Humphreys Alexander (1818-1895). Note his dependence on God and devotion to the Trinity. Can you make this song your own?

*I bind myself today*
*The strong Name of the Trinity,*
*By invocation of the same,*
*The Three in One and One in Three.*
*I bind this day to me for ever*
*By power of faith, Christ's Incarnation;*
*His baptism in Jordan river;*
*His death on Cross for my salvation;*

His bursting from the spiced tomb;
His riding up the heavenly way;
His coming at the day of doom;
I bind unto myself today.

Christ be with me,
Christ within me,
Christ behind me,
Christ before me,
Christ beside me,
Christ to win me,
Christ to comfort and restore me,
Christ beneath me,
Christ above me,
Christ in quiet,
Christ in danger,
Christ in hearts of all that love me,
Christ in mouth of friend and stranger.
I bind unto myself the Name,
The strong Name of the Trinity;
By invocation of the same,
The Three in One, and One in Three.
Of Whom all nature hath creation:
Eternal Father, Spirit, Word:
Praise to the Lord of my salvation,
Salvation is of Christ the Lord.

# WHAT REALLY MATTERS

One of the lessons that parish ministry taught me very early on was that amazing differences can occur between any two people's perceptions of any single event. After any parish event, churchgoers would invariably comment to me on what they enjoyed or did not like about a service. Some would regularly comment on how beautiful the music was and how much they enjoyed the singing. Other members of the congregation would mention the lovely flowers or how the homily touched them. These people seemed to find something to lift their spirits no matter how poorly I felt the service had gone from my point of view. Their comments were always very encouraging for me. Still others would complain that the music was too loud or that there were either too many or too few flowers to adorn the church. They noticed the crying children or found the homily too long or boring. They considered the way other people dressed for church disgraceful, and they took care to let me know. In many cases, their points of view were also very helpful to me when their concerns centered on things that I might improve or change in future services. But I was always amazed at how any two people could have such divergent experiences of the same event.

I imagine that we probably find at any event in life exactly what we are looking for. Those who are looking for beauty in life most likely find it. Those who are looking for other things probably find them. So maybe we need honestly answer the question, "What are we looking for? What really matters?"

We have the example of Solomon from the First Book of Kings. God offers to give Solomon anything at all, and for what is Solomon looking? For what does he ask? An understanding heart. Solomon asks for wisdom to judge right from wrong, that he might live according to God's will. *O LORD, my God, you have made me, your servant, king to succeed my father David; but I am a mere youth, not knowing at all how to act. I serve you in the midst of the people whom you have chosen, a people so vast that it cannot be numbered or counted. Give your servant, therefore, an understanding heart to judge your people and to distinguish right from wrong.* (1 Kings 3:7-9) How many of us, given the same opportunity by God wouldn't have asked for riches or long life or to have those we don't like knocked down a peg or two? Would we have asked for understanding?

In Matthew's gospel, we find the parable of the treasure and the parable of the pearl. These parables challenge us to answer the question, "What is so important in our lives that we'd give up everything to get it?" For Solomon, it was an understanding heart. What would it be for us? Would it be riches? Would it be long life? Would it be beauty? Or would it be faith in Jesus Christ? Saint Peter tells us *there is no salvation through anyone else, nor is there any other name under heaven given to the human race by which we are to be saved* (Acts 4:12). Jesus Christ is the pearl of great price, the treasure worth giving up everything for. Nothing else lasts. Beauty fades, riches get used up, we all get older. Maybe now is the time to focus on what really matters.

# SAVVY SNOWFLAKES

When I was commuting an hour each way to the University of Pittsburgh two nights a week for graduate school, I found myself paying very careful attention to the weather forecasts. There are few pleasures I enjoy more than a quiet walk in the woods after a snowfall, but I hate driving in the snow. I imagine many of you feel the same way. Nonetheless, the snow, like all of God's creations, has a lesson of its own to teach us.

I remember learning in science class when I was a child that every snowflake is different. Most flakes have six sides, owing to the manner in which water crystallizes as it freezes. But no two snowflakes are alike. Each takes on a slightly different shape depending upon the temperature and other conditions present at the time it was formed. Some flakes are very small and simple, comprised of just a few ice crystals. Others may contain more than one hundred crystals in a single flake. It all just depends on what was happening at the time the flake was formed.

Interestingly enough, people are a lot like snowflakes. We come in a variety of shapes and sizes, but we start out surprisingly the same, at least in terms of our molecular structure. What make us different, physically and emotionally, are the conditions in which we were formed. Some would argue that genetics plays a powerful role in predetermining what our physical attributes will be, and there is even evidence that genetics impacts our individual personalities as well. But science also teaches that our genetic composition has been affected by the conditions to which our ancestors adapted across the millennia. So like the snowflake, conditions people face contribute rather significantly to their formation.

In the literature of spirituality, formation is a term that is used, in general, to refer to the process of spiritual growth and development that occurs as we individually respond to the conditions we face in life. This lifelong process is informed by a variety of factors, including life experiences, our emotional responses to these life events and even our knowledge of our faith. What makes this faith knowledge spiritual is the extent to which we integrate that knowledge into our daily responses to life events, either automatically or through purposeful reflection on the faith response called forth by the event.

Like the snowflake, it all depends on the conditions in which we find ourselves at any given moment. A lifetime of conditions has formed us into the persons we are today. Unlike the snowflake, however, God has given us the gift of free will and we choose the impact that life conditions will have on us. Most scholars of spirituality would agree that every life event has formative value. Life events are considered to be formative when we choose to make a faith response that leads us closer to loving God and loving our neighbor — a response that forms us ever more fully in His image. Conditions become deformative when we choose to respond in a way that centers on ourselves, disregarding the grace that is always operative in our lives and the voice of Him who is calling us to ever more fully realize the unique purpose to which He has called us.

Snowflakes. Simple snowflakes. Sometimes the smallest things can remind us of the most profound truths. Each of us has been called into existence by a single word from the mouth of the Father. We are created for a purpose so unique that no one else can accomplish it but us. If we are attentive to the gentle voice of God speaking in and through the events of our lives, we will hear Him speak of our purpose, and we will know what our mission is in life. We will know how to respond to the conditions in our lives.

> *For just as from the heavens*
>> *the rain and snow come down*
> *And do not return there*
>> *till they have watered the earth,*
>> *making it fertile and fruitful,*
> *Giving seed to him who sows*
>> *and bread to him who eats,*
> *So shall my word be*
>> *that goes forth from my mouth;*
> *It shall not return to me void,*
>> *but shall do my will,*
>> *achieving the end for which I sent it* (Is 55:10-11).

Spend some moments in quiet. To what mission do you feel called in life? What is God's purpose for you in the present conditions in your life? Rejoice that He has made you so wonderfully unique, and respect that individuality in others.

# PIVOTAL PLAYERS

In the days before Easter, we recall Jesus' triumphal and final entrance into Jerusalem and our church services present the account of the Passion. We need not wait until Easter to consider the events leading up to the Resurrection. Truthfully, we should think about these pivotal moments in history frequently, because we can learn so much about life and human nature by reflecting on the many scenes and characters who played roles, major and minor, on the stage of Jerusalem in those last days of Jesus' earthly life.

I find that it is very instructive to meditate on the gospel accounts of that first Holy Week over and over again, trying to see the drama unfold through the eyes, ears and emotions of a different eyewitness each time. Jesus, Mary his mother, Mary of Magdala, the disciples, the women of Jerusalem, Pilate, the chief priests, Pharisees, and scribes all provide varied viewpoints from which we can consider this turning point in salvation history. The challenge presented for us in these gospel passages is to enter into this historical event as fully as possible, because this is my history and yours. Our destinies are bound up with this handful of people who lived so long ago, and whose decisions and actions, thoughts and feelings, in accord with the will of the Father, through the loving obedience of the Son and by the grace of the Holy Spirit, made possible the Resurrection, opening the gates of paradise for all of us.

When we look at the ragtag group of persons whose roles in Jesus' Passion the gospels record, we find that those whose fundamental stance was one of dependence on God's providence and receptivity to the working of grace in their lives stand out as the heroes and heroines, while those who jealously attempted to guard their self-interests failed in the long run.

As an exercise in prayer, read one of the Passion narratives when you have some quiet time. Choose some persons presented in the gospel account and reflect upon their points of view as witnesses to the pivotal events of that week so long ago. Formulate some questions to think about: What were these persons' roles in society? Were they part of Jesus' inner circle or an outsider? How might that position have colored their perspectives on the events they witnessed? How did they choose to respond to the things they saw and heard? Were they receptive to God's grace as it unfolded in their lives, or did they try to protect their self-interests? It sounds like hard work, but can actually be a very fruitful form of prayer.

Then honestly consider your own life. Take a hard look at the dramas unfolding on the stage of your experience. Do you see any similarities between yourself and the historical personages about whom you reflected? Are you as receptive as you could be to God's will for you, or do you find yourself trying to protect an agenda that is all your own?

# A MORE GLORIOUS VINTAGE

Back when I was very young, before I was even eight years old, my family lived on Highland Avenue in Aliquippa, Pennsylvania. My aunt and two uncles lived just three doors up the street. I remember that there were always a lot of comings and goings between our two houses. I thought that this was normal and that all families must live this closely. Then, when we moved out to Center Township, things seemed different. We had wonderful neighbors, and as the development in which our house was located grew, more and more nice people moved into the neighborhood. But still, there was something different about our new living situation. The comings and goings weren't there. Times had changed.

People still like to think of themselves as friendly and welcoming. But at least in the natural, spontaneous sense of hospitality, times have changed. Today, most of us would never think of dropping in on our neighbor without calling first. We have enclosed developments, security lighting and locked screened doors. What has happened to the notion of the next door "neighbor?"

This is regrettable, because turning to our neighbor is simply living the Gospel. Jesus taught, *whoever receives you receives me, and whoever receives me receives the one who sent me* (Mt 10: 40). We may think that Christianity is a religion that no longer needs prophets. In a certain sense, this is true, because Jesus is the fulfillment of both the law and the prophets. But if we interpret this narrowly, we're very wrong. Look more closely and you'll see Christ gazing back at you in every face you meet. We cannot allow all of our preoccupation with the business of life to let us forget that just as Christ is priest, prophet and king, we, too, are baptized into that triple mission — especially His prophetic mission, which has everything to do with showing hospitality to our neighbor.

Pondering these notions begs the question, "how much hospitality do we show?" Hospitality is different from entertaining. Entertaining is very often concerned with things — showing the best side of our homes, our yards, our china. Hospitality is about ministering to the needs of others, for food, for water, for companionship, and most of all, for compassion. Ultimately hospitality is about attitude more than plenitude. The 19th century writer Henry David Thoreau expressed this very same concern in these words, *I sat at a table where were rich food and wine in abundance and obsequious attendance, but sincerity and truth were not; and I went away hungry from the inhospitable board… They talked to me of the age of the wine and the fame of the vintage; but I thought of an older, newer, and purer wine, of a more glorious vintage, which they had not got, and could not buy.*

Christian hospitality is much more than cups of coffee, it's about buckets of tolerance and understanding. It quenches the deepest thirst in each of us, and Christ is truly present when we meet him in our acts of compassion to our neighbor.

There's a saying that we often use when we see someone doing something or saying something we think is unjust or unfair: *What goes around, comes around.* I don't think that's quite true. What goes around, my friends, is what we send around. How much compassion, tolerance and understanding are we sending around? Maybe we need to take a closer look at that.

# ATTITUDE ADJUSTMENTS

When we enter into the season of Lent, the words of the prophet Joel resound in churches throughout the world and echo in our hearts:

> Even now, says the LORD,
>> return to me with your whole heart,
>> with fasting, and weeping and mourning;
> Rend your hearts, not your garments,
>> and return to the LORD, your God (Joel 2:12-13).

We hear these words every year, but do they make an impression? The central theme of Lent is one of conversion – renewing our commitment to living our faith. This notion of conversion encompasses both the baptismal and the penitential themes of Lent.

Yet, *even now, says the* LORD,
> *return to me with your whole heart* (Joel 2:12).

While our conversion has been expressed in terms of fasting and making sacrifices – the "give ups" of our childhood – the kind of conversion to which God calls us during Lent is much more fundamental. Making sacrifices is important and can do us physical as well as spiritual good. But too often, we allow the "give up" to become the purpose of our whole Lenten observance, instead of the means to a greater spiritual end. *Rend your hearts, not your garments* (Joel 2:13) the Lord calls out to us. Mere external observance, if it is not a sign of a true inner conversion, is pointless.

If you want to make a change in your life consider, instead of giving something up, adding something faith-based to your approach to daily life. Do you say some sort of prayer in the morning? If not, start. Do you make an examination of conscience before you go to bed? If not, start now! Memorize the Act of Contrition – we should know it by heart and use it at least once a day. Give some thought to your attitude toward life. Mother Teresa had the following inscribed on the wall of her home for children in Calcutta. They are from a book by Kent M. Keith called *Anyway: The Paradoxical Commandments:*

The Paradoxical Commandments

1. People are illogical, unreasonable, and self-centered. *Love them anyway.*

2. If you do good, people will accuse you of selfish ulterior motives. *Do good anyway.*

3. If you are successful, you will win false friends and true enemies. *Succeed anyway.*

4. The good you do today will be forgotten tomorrow. *Do good anyway.*

5. Honesty and frankness make you vulnerable. *Be honest and frank anyway.*

6. The biggest men and women with the biggest ideas can be shot down by the smallest men and women with the smallest minds. *Think big anyway.*

7. People favor underdogs but follow only top dogs. *Fight for*

*a few underdogs anyway.*

8. What you spend years building may be destroyed overnight. *Build anyway.*

9. People really need help but may attack you if you do help them. *Help people anyway.*

10. Give the world the best you have and you'll get kicked in the teeth. *Give the world the best you have anyway.*

Maybe 'rending your hearts' could mean reflecting on Kent Keith's words which so inspired Mother Teresa and applying them with renewed vigor in our lives. Maybe 'giving up' could mean letting go of some of the time we spend in self-indulgence and spending it in prayer. Maybe we will return to the Lord with our whole hearts. Maybe this is the year. Maybe one day soon …

# LOVE'S LOTTERY

*A short time since I danc'd with you, And from that hour lov'd you true; Your pleasing form, your charming air, Might with a fabl'd grace compare; Your accents, so melodious sweet, Still on my ear does seem to beat; And 'tis the first wish of my life, To win my Delia for a wife; Deign, my sweet maid, a line to send, And may love's saint my plea defend.*

The ancient tradition of Valentine's Day, dating to the third century, is based upon the legend of Saint Valentine. One version suggests that Valentine was a priest who was martyred for marrying young couples despite the Emperor Claudius II's ban on Christian marriages. Since then, Valentine has been regarded by tradition as the patron saint of lovers. In the middle ages, it was believed the birds chose their mates on February 14th, which became an auspicious day for sending greetings of love to one's heart's desire. Some even demanded a response, like the verse above which dates from the American colonial era.

As I recall it, Valentine's Day was always fun when I was a child. Every year, we raided my parents' closets to purloin their shoeboxes for the making of the annual Valentine box. These were always judged at school, with the nicest winning a prize. I was amazed at some of the extremes to which my classmates went in order to win. Mine usually involved the use of aluminum foil and lots of white, pink and red construction paper hearts. I never won the prize for the best Valentine box, but that never seemed to matter once the box started filling up. Every year there was a surprise — sometimes a Valentine from someone quite unexpected; some years no Valentine when I was desperately hoping for one in particular. One just never knew in the lottery of love, but we sure gambled hard.

To be in love is a great gift, and perhaps the proverb that it is better to have loved and lost than to have never loved at all is true. But if so, it is only true insofar as we learn to value love. Otherwise, we fail to recognize the great gift of love that we have already received. We don't have to wait for Valentines for love poetry. God speaks continually to our hearts. He woos us saying:

How beautiful you are, how pleasing,
    my love, my delight! (Song 7:7)
The Lord pleads with us:
Set me as a seal on your heart,
    as a seal on your arm (Song 8:6).

If you are in love, realize that your love is a treasure and act accordingly. Let your sweetheart know you value his or her presence in your life. Look for verses from the Song of Songs to express your love. What could be more beautiful than the inspired Scripture for expressing your feelings?

If you are not in love at the moment, don't let it get you down. If you haven't found someone special, maybe God's giving you time to get to know yourself, and to learn to love your-self better first. After all, you do have a love relationship with the Lord. Take a look at the Song of Songs. Its title means "the greatest of all songs," and it is understood to express the great love that Christ has for his bride, the Church, and even, accord-ing to Saint Bernard, depicts the deep union between Jesus and the individual soul. Celebrate that love relationship by spending some extra time in prayer, basking in the arms of your Lord.

# BEING AND BECOMING

As we enter November, the world around us begins to settle in for its winter rest. The frosts have blighted the flowers and as I sit in my rocker, the tree outside my window, so vibrant with color just two weeks ago has faded and is all but bare. We have enjoyed what may well be the last balmy days of Indian summer. I cannot help but find myself reflecting on the mystery of life and the purpose of being. In the midst of it all stands my tree — an icon of the blessing of our creation and of the mystery of our existence, our life, as Saint Paul describes it, *hidden with Christ in God* (Col 3:3).

Thomas Merton once wrote, *a tree gives glory to God by being a tree. For in being what God means it to be, it is obeying Him. It "consents" so to speak, to His creative love.* Merton goes on to say, *the more a tree is like itself, the more it is like Him. If it tried to be like something else which it was never intended to be, it would be less like God and therefore it would give Him less glory ... this particular tree will give glory to God by spreading out its roots in the earth and raising its branches into the air and the light in a way that no other tree before or after it ever did or will do.* (*New Seeds of Contemplation*, 29). Is not the same true of us as individual souls?

We are fortunate to begin the month of November each year with the feasts of All Saints and All Souls. These two glorious feasts give us hope by showing us, just as vividly as the colors of the trees in autumn, how beautiful life is and how full of possibilities. Can we be saints? Absolutely. We need only consent to be the persons God calls us to be. Merton goes on to say, *for me to be a saint means to be myself. Therefore, the problem of sanctity and salvation is in fact the problem of finding out who I am and of discovering my true self. Trees and animals have no problem. God makes them what they are without consulting them, and they are perfectly satisfied. With us it is different. God leaves us free to be whatever we like. We can be ourselves or not, as we please.* (*New Seeds*, 31).

In my work with college students over the years, I have been privileged to witness their individual odysseys as they work to discover who it is that God is calling them to be. Very rarely does the young man or woman bear a very strong resemblance on graduation day to the boy or girl who showed up at Freshman Orientation four years earlier. Sometimes I look at them and wonder what I must have appeared like when I was developing through my college years. In my case it took me until the age of thirty to consent to be the person God has called me to be — and even now, I sometimes feel that my response is incomplete.

Why is it so difficult for us to consent fully to God's will in our lives? I think that part of the difficulty stems from the fact that in order to truly open ourselves to God's plan, we must give up our delusions about ourselves, about our abilities, our talents and our gifts. We cannot fully consent to God's will in our lives until we are truly humble and happy with ourselves as God has made us. As long as we concern ourselves with climbing the ladder, with gaining wealth and with others' opinions, we will never be truly free to become our real selves. The Christian vocation is not an easy one. We must consent to die little deaths to our delusions about ourselves. Like the tree outside my window, for which each winter holds the budding promise of a new, vibrant spring of regrowth, every time we let go of a false notion about ourselves, we blossom more beautiful, more true, more free.

# 7

# GRATITUDE

*We thank you, God, we give thanks;*
*we call upon your name,*
*declare your wonderful deeds. (Ps 75:2)*

Harvest time at Home, Indiana County, Pennsylvania.  Photo by Kim Metzgar.

# DANCE ON A DOCK

One summer I vacationed with my sisters and their families in Deep Creek, Maryland. It was great. It took two townhouses and an apartment to house us for the week, but we were right on the lake. It was so peaceful in the mornings to pray my Office, sipping my coffee and watching the ducks ambling by on the water. I woke early every day, bright eyed, if not exactly bushy tailed, ready for a new day full of adventure. I stayed up late into the night. Our days were full; so full, in fact, that it is difficult for me to say what the high point of the week was. It might have been white water rafting with my nephews, David and Brian, and my nieces, Lyndley and Erin. Our raft team really worked well together. It could have been canoeing with my brother-in-law Scott. Perhaps it was watching my sister Michaleen trying to manage her horse when we went riding. I'm pretty sure that it wasn't when I fell and sustained a "brutal" back injury at the hand of my oldest sister, Denise, who tried to push me off the dock on the very first day. But I didn't mind, and it didn't slow me down a bit — it was all in fun.

I think that what made the vacation so restful spiritually

and emotionally, if not physically, was that we played. We adults played every day; together and with our children. We swam and we laid out on the dock in the sun, listening to music and frolicking with the kids in the water. We took turns on the speed boat we had rented for the week; some of us water skiing, some tubing, some just enjoying the ride. We miniature golfed, we played cards, we played volleyball and went hiking. We danced like fools on the dock in the broad daylight with our children, and didn't care who saw us. We went shopping and watched artisans crafting, watched TV together, read our books together and ate our meals — together. The week was anything but restful, and yet I am refreshed.

There was a commercial on the television that I saw before I left for vacation. Perhaps that's why I played so hard. The commercial started with a little boy, about the age of four or five, who asks his dad how much money he makes in a week. His father is shaving and ignores the question. In the next scene, he asks his father how much he earns in a day. The father, reading his newspaper, casts a frustrated look at the television viewer over the top of his paper. Again he tries to ask his father the question, but he appears to be watching television and waves the boy off. In the final scene, the father looks in on him when he's getting ready for bed and asks his son why he's been so concerned about money. The child responds that he's been saving up and shows his dad a handful of change. Then, the boy asks if that's enough money to buy some time with dad.

It was a very powerful commercial and it evokes a very visceral bittersweet response.

Like the commercial, my week with my family had its bittersweet moments, too. One of these was when, after the white water rafting adventure, I casually asked my godson, Brian, who had just graduated from college that spring, how he liked his job. Brian launched into an animated discussion of environmental safety testing in industry and OSHA standards, which I didn't entirely follow. But I realized that he was now a grown man, no longer the toddler wrestling with me and his twin sister Meghan on my parents' living room floor when I was home on break from college. Another bittersweet moment was when I sat down with my nephew David and his girlfriend to talk about their getting married. It was very difficult for me to try to conduct a "professional" discussion. All that I could see when I looked at him was the toddler who used to hoist himself up on his tiptoes so that he could get his face over the top of his play-pen to make "fish face" at us.

Our children are precious. They grow up so quickly. I just can't imagine how we can afford to waste a single minute with them. Sure, we're all busy. We work hard and at the end of the day we are exhausted. I know all about that. But I also know how much I have given up in choosing religious life. So I try not to waste opportunities to see my nieces and nephews. You shouldn't either. When we're retired, it will be too late. The children will be grown and gone.

Take some time to play with your kids, your grandchildren or your nieces or your nephews. Dance on a dock. Play some ball. Read them a story. The time spent is an investment in the future and a blessing in the present. Be like Christ who said, "*Let the children come to me and do not prevent them; for the kingdom of God belongs to such as these*" (Lk 18:16). You will find yourself refreshed.

# VACATION IN VERMONT

I had the rare opportunity to travel to northern Vermont to preside at a wedding for a very close friend of our family. I left after I finished teaching my college class the Wednesday before and stayed overnight in Wilkes-Barre, and then continued on the next day until I got to Stowe, where the wedding was to take place.

The drive was beautiful, especially when I got into New York and Vermont. The mountains were absolutely lush, a deep green, and I felt free as a bird zooming down the highway. I had never been to Vermont. The drive took me through some villages that had all the charm for which New England is known. I was mesmerized. Saint Thomas Aquinas argued that God's existence could be proved by observing both the beauty and order of the universe. On the one hand, the beauty of creation points to its creator, and on the other, the orderliness of the world suggests an intelligent designer — that is to say, the universe did not fall into place by accident. Judging by the unspoiled beauty of the mountains of Vermont, Saint Thomas knew what he was talking about. Quite without my intending it, the trip took on a spiritual aspect for me, simply by exposure to the beauty of nature.

We were staying at the Von Trapp family lodge, the home where the family from *The Sound of Music* settled after they fled Austria before the Nazi occupation. I could easily see why the Von Trapps chose to settle in Vermont. It reminded me very much of the Austrian Alps without the snow peaks. The terrain is very much like that surrounding Salzburg. Much of our free time during the weekend was spent studying the various photographs and historical information displayed about the family. We even visited the family burial ground and saw the graves of Georg and Maria Von Trapp. Two of the children still live on the grounds, and the lodge is run by Fraulein Maria's grandson, Johannes. For my sisters and me, who were accustomed to watching *The Sound of Music* when it was on television every year, the weekend was quite exciting.

One of the most delightful parts of the trip for me was being able to spend time with my family. For the first time in decades, my parents, five sisters and I were all together like we were when we were little. Husbands and children had been left at home, so it was just us. Of course we missed my brothers-in-law and the kids, but it was a nice nostalgic feeling being all together around the breakfast table once again. My parents reveled in it and so did we. It was just like being kids again, and we so enjoyed each other's company! We laughed and danced and laughed some more. It was gifted time, and we recognized it and appreciated it as such.

The wedding went perfectly. Our neighbor Rebecca, who was the bride, looked stunningly beautiful, and the whole affair was wonderful, tasteful and elegant. A great time was had by all.

On the drive back home, alone and reflecting on the trip, I listened to some country western music. There was a song, I don't know by whom or what it was called. In its lyrics, though, there was a reference to life just happening while we're waiting for our dreams to come to true. I wish I knew what that song was called or who sings it, because I think it makes an excellent point: it is probably rather rare when our life turns out the way we dreamed it would when we were kids. But does that matter? Is that so bad? Of course we have to make plans, that's the nature of human existence, but perhaps what we really need to do is to appreciate and enjoy what life offers us right here and now. My family and I certainly did that in Vermont.

Take some time to reflect on your life as it is today. Don't obsess about your future plans. Look for the signs of God's presence and His many gifts to you. Remember, even if things haven't worked out the way you dreamed they might, *Whoever finds his life will lose it, and whoever loses his life for my sake will find it* (Mt 10:39). By focusing less on future plans and more on Christ present to us in the here and now, we discover the beauty of our authentic identity.

# HEARTH AND HOME

In October, I spent a week at home with my parents. It was a wonderful retreat for me. I rested and enjoyed their company. It was healing for me just to be at home where I grew up. To look out the kitchen window every morning and see the beautiful colors of the leaves was a real treat. That is one of my greatest treasures, for I can feel so close to God when I reflect on the beauty of His creation.

Aside from desperately needed rest and relaxation, the week held a number of delightful surprises as well. One of these was a week long project that provided time for my mom and me to be together. My mother was just about to start making my niece RaeAnn's Halloween costume when I arrived. Rainie, who was four years old, wanted to go trick-or-treating as a princess, and so a gown, girdle and cape had to be created. With six children, and five of them daughters, my mother's sewing machine was never idle when we were growing up. Consequently, my mother made sure that all of her children, even me, knew how to operate it, if only marginally. It was one of the ways that Mom ensured that we would be able to fend for ourselves in adulthood. So I got the dubious pleasure of helping her. We worked on the costume for a part of each day.

Because I have this tendency to become obsessive when I am working on any project, Mom and I made a deal that we would keep our perspective, but my perfectionism got the better of me. Even though the most often quoted statement of the week was "It's only a costume," when I returned to the Abbey, Rainie had everything she needed to be a beautiful princess in red and gold satin, complete with a crown. The visit was restful for me, but Mom was no doubt exhausted by my "help."

Another treat was spending time with my sister Ladonna. I had been so busy during September and the first week of October that I had fallen behind on birthdays, so Donn and I spent a day out for lunch and shopping. The day culminated in a trip back to our *alma mater* for the Friday night football game. Our team won by a narrow margin, but the highlights for me were watching my niece Lauren, a senior cheerleader, and watching the high school band's halftime show. I learned that high school cheerleading has become a gymnastic sport. I was so proud of Lauren. She's really talented. Her twin sister Lyndley is also quite an athlete, but gave up cheerleading a few years back for cross country and basketball. It was quite nostalgic for me to watch the band. I spent hundreds of hours in high school working on halftime shows myself. It was a pleasure to see that the band was every bit as good as we were then.

My whole family gathered for the local wedding reception of our friends whose wedding I celebrated in Vermont on September 1. It was a lovely evening. Since the bride's father teaches at the high school, many of the faculty were invited. I got to visit with many of my former teachers. It was a wonderful evening, spent with family and lifelong friends.

It is really important not to lose sight of the giftedness of everyday life. Each of the events of my week at home was perfectly ordinary, but to me each was special because I recognized it as God's gift to me. So, I returned rested and joyful.

Take a long look around you. Make a list of the gentle gifts that God sends your way each day. Then pray. Pray a prayer of thanksgiving and pray a prayer for each person who brings you a simple joy. Then take time to tell them — and don't underestimate the difference your words make in spreading God's peace. In the Hebrew Scriptures, Naomi gives us an example when she tells her daughters-in-law, Orpah and Ruth, *May the LORD be kind to you as you were . . . to me* (Ruth 1:8). And the wisdom of the proverbs teaches:

> *like golden apples in silver settings*
> *are words spoken at the proper time* (Prov 25:11).

# FOUR-LEGGED FRIENDS

When the weather turns warm, I find myself outside doing work in my garden, just soaking up the sun and warm breeze, and loving life. Of course, I do not work alone; one of my cat pals is often nearby. I find it a blessing to have a pet and to spend time with him outdoors. It teaches me a great deal, and argues for the benefit of having an animal friend. Crystal Ward Kent, in her book, *The Journey*, writes of the path of discovery and joy upon which we embark when an animal comes into our lives, be that entry planned or unexpected. Ms. Ward Kent writes,

*When you bring a pet into your life, you begin a journey — a journey that will bring you more love and devotion than you have ever known, yet also test your strength and courage. If you allow, the journey will teach you many things, about life, about yourself, and most of all, about love. You will come away changed forever, for one soul cannot touch another without leaving its mark. Along the way, you will learn much about savoring life's simple pleasures – jumping in leaves, snoozing in the sun, the joys of puddles, and even the satisfaction of a good scratch behind the ears.*

*If you spend much time outside, you will be taught how to truly experience every element, for no rock, leaf, or log will go unexam-*

ined, no rustling bush will be overlooked, and even the very air will be inhaled, pondered, and noted as being full of valuable information. Your pace may be slower — except when heading home to the food dish — but you will become a better naturalist, having been taught by an expert in the field.

Too many times we hike on automatic pilot, our goal being to complete the trail rather than enjoy the journey. We miss the details — the colorful mushrooms on the rotting log, the honeycomb in the old maple snag, the hawk feather caught on a twig. Once we walk as a dog does, we discover a whole new world. We stop, we browse the landscape, we kick over leaves, peek in tree holes, look up, down, all around. And we learn what any dog knows: that God has created a marvelously complex world that is full of surprises, that each cycle of the seasons bring ever changing wonders, each day an essence all its own.

The book of Genesis tells us that when God created the universe, He gave man all of the various animals and birds for his enjoyment. On the sixth day of creation, God said *"Let the earth bring forth all kinds of living creatures: cattle, creeping things, and wild animals of all kinds." And so it happened: God made all kinds of wild animals, all kinds of cattle, and all kinds of creeping things of the earth. God saw how good it was* (Gen 1:24-25). What stands out when I read this passage of scripture is that *God saw how good it was.* Perhaps one part of this goodness is the fact that our pets cause us to slow down, and as Ward Kent points out, notice the beauty of the creation that we so often rush right by in our hurry to do more "important" things. While I certainly complete fewer of my garden chores when one of my feline friends is working by my side, I find that I do get to know my garden much, much more intimately. Because my cat prods me to see the garden from his perspective, at soil level, I notice the details of my garden and the subtleties of the ecosystem that I have helped to develop. When I take the time to notice the finer points of my garden, those which can only been seen at ground level, I find myself pondering the miracle that God has wrought in creation, and I am amazed that I have been blessed to play a small role in co-creating it with Him. Such observation, such reflection, is in itself a very powerful form of prayer, for all prayer has as its goal the turning of the heart toward God. When our hearts are moved by simple beauty, our souls are stirred in what may well be the purest form of praise, and I cannot help but think that such moments restore us to the relationship God had in mind for us from the beginning.

Don't let this season pass you by. Get outside even for a little while to see the signs of God's love all around you. If you have a pet, take him out with you and watch him closely. Notice the details that your pet points out to you. You will learn new things about the world around you and God's bountiful blessings, and your relationship with your Creator will grow stronger as He calls you back to the beginning.

# THE WISE WOMAN

As I celebrated one of those landmark birthdays that we all tend to dread, it made me wonder about my life and what I thought I would have accomplished by the time I had reached the age of 40. When I reflect on what my dreams were when I was graduating from college so many years ago, I could easily allow myself to be depressed because I haven't really accomplished many of the things that I dreamed for my life. But I guess that I have accomplished different things and I know that my life is a very happy one.

Most of us know and have visited a family member or friend who is elderly. It was my happy privilege when I was a parochial vicar to visit each month my homebound parishioners, most of whom were quite advanced in age.

I recall one woman in particular. When I visited her for the first time, I immediately sensed that I was in the presence of person who seemed, at least in my estimation, to be profoundly wise. This woman was a living paradox: at once almost overwhelmingly astute yet adorned in utter simplicity. This was someone who would have been the village wise-woman had she lived in another time and place.

She typically received me in her kitchen, which was always warm and welcoming. In all seasons dried herbs could be found at hand, which lent the room an air of a medieval apothecary's shop. It was warm and earthy and smelled spicy. Oddly, I was always humbled in her presence, yet perfectly comfortable.

Many were the lessons that she taught me during our brief conversations over the three years that I visited with her. One lesson that I gleaned from many conversations with her was about the nature of growing older. She would often share memories with me. After several months, I noticed a pattern. Not once in all our visits would she comment about her failing health or her aches and pains and not once did she share sadness with me. I recall studying her wrinkled visage one day and realizing that she must surely have known her share of heartache, but that she only talked about happy memories. One time I even dared to ask her about this. She told me that she had indeed known sadness and hard times, like anyone else, she added, but that she didn't see her life defined in terms of those experiences. When she looked back on her long life, she told me, she chose to see instead, the many, many blessings she had received.

When we have any experience, whether that be of life or even of printed text, our perceptions are colored by the previous experiences we have had and the concerns with which we are struggling at that moment in our lives. For me, the wise-woman taught the importance of remembering that each day we have a choice to make. We can choose to let the difficulties in our lives define us — or we can choose to be happy. Either way the choice is ours. We may not have a say in the hand we're dealt in life, but we always have a choice in how we play it. As Christians, we're supposed to live our lives from a stance of thanksgiving and hope. That being the case, it would seem logical to me that we would recognize that each day is a gift, and we can choose to discern God's will and find happiness in each moment, regardless of how troubled it might seem. God stands by our side, and my wise friend illustrated that elegantly.

I certainly don't have the money, prestige or position that I dreamed I would have when I reached 40. After all, I left college a young man full of ambition, with dreams of power and success. Every day I thank God that he didn't give me what I hoped for back when I was young — and foolish. In His great kindness, He gave me much, much more. I'm richer in happiness than I ever imagined, and I thank those I serve each day for being a part of that happiness.

If you take a look at your life, you will no doubt find plenty of reasons to be thankful, hopeful and happy.

*Happy the man who finds wisdom,*
*the man who gains understanding!*
*For her profit is better than profit in silver,*
*and better than gold is her revenue;*
*She is more precious than corals,*
*and none of your choice possessions can compare with her.*
*Long life is in her right hand,*
*in her left are riches and honor;*
*Her ways are pleasant ways,*
*and all her paths are peace* (Prov 3:13-17).

# THE BLAME GAME

Early in my career as a college financial director, I was involved in a car accident as I was arriving at work. I had been distracted by a bus while I was pulling into the parking lot at the college and did not see my colleague stop at the gate ahead of me. I dented his bumper and damaged mine. It wasn't a serious accident, but it left me completely frazzled. Not surprisingly, later that morning while I was working on a student's financial aid package, I made a calculation error because I was still distracted by the fender-bender. The result was that I authorized a grant to a student who was technically ineligible for funding.

I did not notice my error until the end of the day when I was cleaning my desk and organizing the student files I had worked on that day to be returned to the main file room. By then, however, it was too late to easily correct the error. The data sheet had already been logged into the computer system and notification to the student had already gone out in the day's mail.

Even though it was a small matter, I found myself very angry as I walked to the parking lot, arguing with myself and with God the whole way home. Why had He allowed me to become distracted that morning? Now, not only did I have to deal with the car repair issue, but I had to take back money that I had awarded. How was I going to explain that to the student, or for that matter, to my boss? We were required to check and double-check our work before signing any documents. Apparently, I had failed to do so.

The next morning, I took the student's file to my boss and explained the mistake I had made. I remember he sat back in his chair and looked at me over his spectacles. I was fortunate to work under the guidance of a good man, one of the best in the business, but my boss was strict with us as well. He demanded excellence. But he was also a very wise man. I learned that morning, that his practice was always to hold some college funds in reserve. Rather than making me write to the student, withdrawing the funds I had awarded in error, he simply swapped some reserve funds for the federal grant I had awarded. He did, however, remind me somewhat sternly about the necessity of checking my work and remaining focused.

About a week later, one of the clerical staff appeared at my office door with a piece of notebook paper in hand. The student whom I had mistakenly given a grant had returned her award letter accepting the grant, and had written me a thank you note. In her note, she explained how she had reluctantly applied for financial aid, thinking that she would not be eligible to receive any funding because of her husband's income. But she went on to say that despite the fact that their family income looked promising on paper, by the time she and her husband dealt with the normal expenses of living, there barely was enough left to make tuition for her nursing program at the college. She had applied for a grant as a last resort. She and her husband were tapped out financially. They were unable to even consider loan assistance. If she had not received a grant, she would have had to drop out of her nursing program. As it turned out, my mistake enabled the student to pay for her last semester of nursing school.

So often, like I did in my foolishness, we want to blame God when things go wrong in our lives. But I think that perhaps we need to take a hard look at situations before we start playing the blame game. Most of the time, when something goes wrong in our lives, it can be traced to a bad decision that we made or a mistake, like mine, that happened through our own carelessness. These sorts of events have very little to do with God's will. More often than not, our problems arise from our own choices. Rather than interfere with our free will, God seizes the opportunity to make good come out of the situation. What was unusual about my experience in this case was that I actually got to see the good that came out of my mistake. Most of us never do. But that does not mean that God has not wrought some sort of good from our misfortunes.

When bad things happen to us, we get to make a choice. We can wallow in sorrow and self-pity, or we can choose to look at the situation through the eyes of faith. To do so is a great grace, but I do not believe that it is an extraordinary grace. Rather, the grace to trust God to make good come out of the messiness of life is available to all of us, all the time. The ancients understood this wisdom, and taught it faithfully to their young:

*Commit your way to the LORD;*
   *trust that God will act*
*And make your integrity shine like the dawn,*
   *your vindication like noonday* (Ps 37:5-6)

and elsewhere:

> *trust in the L*ORD *with all your heart,*
> *on your own intelligence rely not*
> *In all your ways be mindful of him,*
> *and he will make straight your paths* (Prov 3:5-6)

The next time something goes wrong in your life, instead of blaming God, take a leap of faith and try thanking Him. Make an act of trust that He is present in your situation. Thank Him for the unseen good that only He can make come out of it, and trust the Lord to work little miracles along the way.

# PRAYERFUL PASTIMES

Few activities in life bring me more joy than gardening. Though I am certainly no sophisticated landscaper, I love to get my hands dirty working with plants, even if limited to a few pots and window boxes.

My grandmother instilled in me my love for working with plants. Grandma Farland's house had countless potted plants, and her yard was a virtual botanical garden. She had it all – peonies in three colors, lilies of the valley, white pine trees, tulip trees, roses, spring bulb flowers. Grandma loved hyacinths in particular, and purple lilacs. Every year in early May, we would get cut lilacs from Grandma's lilac bush. A lot of years have passed since Grandma went home to be with her Lord, but I can't help but think of her whenever I see a lilac bush. In fact, because my mother feels the same way I do, I got her a lilac bush for her yard a few years back. Some traditions just have to be carried on.

Perhaps one reason that I find gardening so enjoyable, even with my limited talent for it, is that working with plants requires me to slow down and take a close look at what God has created. The intricacy of even a simple woodland violet is really quite awe inspiring if we but take a moment to consider it as an individual gift directly from the hand of God. Gardening puts me in touch with the every day miracles of life. I feel closer to God when I'm working with plants – and so, the joy I experience becomes a form of prayer, an act of worship.

We tend to think of prayer as a sit-down activity – one that requires quiet and calm, concentration and solemnity. Perhaps some forms of prayer are like that, but if we wait for the perfect conditions, we could be missing a lot of opportunities to pray and we might be missing the whole point of prayer. Prayer is simply time spent with God. It matters not where or when or even how we pray. It matters only that we pray.

For me, praying outdoors on a walk or working in my small courtyard garden is an act of worship, of co-creating with the Trinity, of glorifying Him who has called me and all of creation into being. It just makes sense for me. After all, Adam and Eve, the first people to pray, did so in a garden.

Think about starting a small garden. Even if you don't have a lot of space, a couple of planters or pots on your patio or windowsill can open a doorway where you can encounter the living God. Spend some moments reflecting on the wondrous design and engineering in simple plants, and be amazed. Allow your heart to turn to God in thanksgiving.

# GREEN BLESSINGS

During Holy Week and Easter week in the spring of 2003, I was fortunate to have some time off from my work at the Clelian Heights School for Exceptional Children and a few days off from graduate studies at the University of Pittsburgh as well. With the beautiful weather we had, I found myself free to enjoy some time to work in my garden, preparing it for the summer months. The winter had been a hard season, and I found that some of my favorite perennials didn't survive the bitter cold. But that provided me with an opportunity to peruse the garden centers for new ideas. Taking a risk, I planted some petunias and snapdragons, though there might yet be an overnight frost. Then I got daring and decided to try growing some herbs and even some cherry tomatoes. I have never had much success with vegetables, but I thought that perhaps this year I might get lucky. As it turned out, they did beautifully.

What a blessed pleasure it is to work with the soil! I found myself reveling in the beauty of God's creation and reflecting on the cycle of the seasons and the joyous mystery of the resurrection. It was a wonderful way to celebrate Easter. Christ is risen! Indeed He is risen!

It would never suffice simply to get my hands dirty among

my plants, for life is holy. By this I mean that all of life is an occasion for giving praise to God from Whose hand we freely receive each and every day as gift, along with all the simple joys that each day brings. Consequently, I found myself seeking out prayers that might express my gratitude for the quiet healing moments I spent alone in my garden. I found that Psalm 104 aptly portrays God's gracious goodness in creation.

*Bless the Lord, my soul!*
*Lord, my God, you are great indeed!*
*You made springs to flow into channels*
*that wind among the mountains.*
*They give drink to every beast of the field;*
*here wild asses quench their thirst.*
*Beside them the birds of heaven nest;*
*among the branches they sing.*
*You water the mountains from your palace;*
*by your labor the earth abounds.*
*You raise grass for the cattle*
*and plants for our beasts of burden.*
*You bring bread from the earth.*
*and wine to gladden our hearts.*
*Oil to make our faces gleam,*
*food to build our strength.*
*The trees of the Lord drink their fill,*
*the cedars of Lebanon, which you planted.*
*There the birds build their nests;*
*junipers are the home of the stork.*
*The high mountains are for wild goats;*
*the rocky cliffs, a refuge for badgers.* (Ps 104: 1, 10-18).

I believe that when we work the soil, we partake in God's recreating anew the beauty of Eden. These are sacred moments, and should be properly revered as such. Our ability to share in such graced times is a blessing indeed, and should be hallowed with prayer.

May you enjoy a wonderful season among the plants you help God to grow, be they in simple pots or flowing fields, indoors or outside. May they bring you much beauty and joy. May you also find your gardening work to be a blessed time with your Creator. Allow Him to bring you His blessed peace.

# COAT OF MANY COLORS

When I was a young man, just out of college, I took a position as a financial aid director at an inner-city community college. Many of the students I served were unemployed, displaced from jobs in the dying steel industry or trying to break the cycle of poverty that had bound their families to public assistance or welfare for generations. I loved the work, which enabled me to help people of all ages to gain access to training that might offer them a better life.

While I can remember days from my youth when money was tight, my family was never really poor. So when I first found myself working with people who truly had need, I was at a loss to appreciate their circumstances. The students taught me about what being poor really means. It was not unusual to find students who were "temporarily" living in their cars, or in buildings that had been condemned. One of my first clients needed my help finding an agency that would help him to get glasses so that he could read his textbooks. Although I worked a part-time job to help pay for my own college costs, I could not imagine trying to study while struggling with housing, food or healthcare needs.

Most of the students I served did not speak Standard American English. Their manners were not polished, and they had little clue to the finer nuances of the upper middle class etiquette in which I had been socialized growing up. But working with those who were financially poor, I came to realize that poverty has many definitions. Not all of them have to do with a shortage of money. What I came to gradually learn from my students is that being financially poor does not render one second or third class. Being financially poor means that one does not have money, but oddly enough, I came to learn that dignity does not come from having money. What the students I served taught me was that being rich is more a function of the quality of our human relationships than the quality of our bank accounts. Being rich is more a matter of our stance toward life than economic resources.

I have been a fan of country music singer Dolly Parton since I was a teenager. When I came to know about some of my students' lives, I was reminded of one of her songs, *Coat of Many Colors*. In that song, Dolly tells of a time when she was a little girl and her family was really poor. She didn't have a coat for school, but someone had given her mother a bag of rags. Her mother, as the song tells, sewed the rags together to make Dolly a coat. As she worked on the coat, she told Dolly the story from Genesis of Joseph, and his coat of many colors. When Dolly wore her coat to school, the other children made fun of her. The lesson that stuck with me from that song is found in the final two stanzas:

*Oh I couldn't understand it*
*For I felt I was rich.*
*And I told them of the love*

*My momma sewed in every stitch.*
*And I told 'em all the story*
*Momma told me while she sewed.*
*And how my coat of many colors*
*Was worth more than all their clothes.*

*But they didn't understand it*
*And I tried to make them see*
*That one is only poor*
*Only if they choose to be.*
*Now I know we had no money*
*But I was rich as I could be*
*In my coat of many colors*
*My momma made for me.*
*Made just for me.*

When we find ourselves focusing on all that we don't have in life, we would do well to remember the lesson from Dolly's song. We are only poor if we choose to see ourselves as such. Wealth does not come from having money; nor does it come from accumulating lots of stuff. Real wealth and true happiness are found simply in recognizing that all of creation, all of life, is freely given from the hand of God. So the next time we feel inclined toward complaining or self-pity over what is lacking in our lives, perhaps we would do well to stop and consider the gifts laying right under our noses: the people in our lives, the roof over our heads and the beauty of creation all around us.

*Can any of you by worrying add a single moment to your life-span? ... Learn from the way the wild flowers grow ... If God so clothes the grass of the field, which grows today and is thrown into the oven tomorrow, will he not much more provide for you?* (Mt 6:27-28, 30)

# EACH NEW DAY IS A GIFT

Early June is the time for high school graduations. In reflecting on what advice I could offer to graduating young parishioners, I came across the following story in a book titled, *God's Little Devotional Book.* I think it makes a valid point, and one well worth considering.

*Several centuries ago, the emperor of Japan commissioned a Japanese artist to paint a particular species of bird for him. Months passed, then years. Finally, the Emperor went personally to the artist's studio to ask for an explanation.*

*The artist set a blank canvas on the easel and within fifteen minutes, had created a painting of a bird. It was a masterpiece! The Emperor, admiring both the painting and the artist's great skill, asked why there had been such a long delay.*

*The artist then went from cabinet to cabinet in his studio. He pulled from them armloads of drawings of feathers, tendons, wings, feet, claws, eyes, beaks – virtually every aspect of a bird, from virtually every angle. He placed these silently before the Emperor, who nodded in understanding. The magnificence of any "whole" can never be greater than the magnificence of any singular detail.*

*To have an excellent life, strive for an excellent year. Within that year, strive for an excellent month, and within that month, strive for an excellent day. Within that day, strive for an excellent hour. An excellent life is the sum of many excellent moments!*

It seems to me that all of us could benefit from reflecting on the teaching of this story. Excellence does not consist of being rich or famous. It does not consist of having the best job, or the biggest house or the most money in the bank. It does not consist of being popular or even of being smart. It consists in making the best use of each moment of life. It consists in doing the best we can with each day, recognizing that each new day is a gift that we receive freely from the hand of God. If we want to live an excellent life, we just have to do the best we can with each new day, living in the constant awareness that we have been gifted with another day, and responding in gratitude to the Giver of all gifts.

# GOD'S GIFT TO US

One of my most enduring memories from childhood is the way my mother would prepare our Thanksgiving meal. By the time we'd get home from school on Wednesday, there would be at least four pies cooling on the kitchen counter. Mom would have three pumpkin, but the last, made for her father, would be minced meat. "Tom," the hapless turkey for the feast, would be thawing on a large platter in the refrigerator. After dinner, Mom would let me help break up the bread for the stuffing, while she worked on the cranberry salad. Nobody makes stuffing or cranberry salad like my Mom!

Thanksgiving morning, Tom would already be in the oven and the kitchen, warm and cozy, would smell great by the time my sisters and I came downstairs in our pajamas to watch the parades on TV. The highlight of the parade would be at the end when Santa Claus made his appearance. Later in the afternoon, Grandma and Grandpap Farland would arrive for the dinner, which I got to help serve once I got big enough.

A long corridor of years divides the man I have become from the simple boy who looked forward with such delight to Thanksgiving Day. I suspect most of us could say the same. Our lives today are a great deal different from our childhood, and life in this New World has radically changed since the Separatist "pilgrims" gathered to celebrate the first Thanksgiving Day. But the essence of the day is one that can never grow old, never grow tired, never become irrelevant. The pilgrims gathered to thank Almighty God for the gifts of food and shelter, for the gifts of love and friendship, for the gift of His Providence. Thanksgiving was a time when my parents took care to very gently remind us that we are not *entitled* to anything in this life. Everything we have and all those we love are God's generous gifts to us.

Take some time to reflect on the sights, sounds and smells of Thanksgiving, including good fellowship. Consider God's generosity in your life:

*Give thanks to God, bless his name;*
*good indeed is the Lord,*
*Whose love endures forever,*
*whose faithfulness lasts through every age.* (Ps 100:4-5).

# 8
# RESPITE

*... Come away by yourselves to a deserted place and rest a while ...* **(Mk 6:31)**

Geese on Keystone Lake, Keystone State Park, Derry Township,
Westmoreland County, Pennsylvania. Photo by Kim Metzgar.

# RUMMAGING FOR RUDOLPH

Until I was eight years old, my family lived in Aliquippa on Highland Avenue. There were just two houses between ours and the house where my father grew up, so naturally, we spent a lot of time in my Grandma Kanfush's house. She died when I was only three years old, so I don't have much of a memory of her. But she had a Christmas decoration that I just loved. It was a velveteen reindeer — red, with silver sparkle antlers. There was a little silver bell on a chain around his neck. Typical tyke that I was, I called him Rudolph. When I wasn't at her house, Rudolph decorated the windowsill in the her kitchen, but whenever I visited, she'd take him down and I got to play with Rudolph. I played with him so much that Grandma finally gave him to me to keep for my very own. Rudolph is the only memory I have from my Grandmother.

When he made the move down the street to our house, Rudolph became a fixture under our Christmas tree. He could be found proudly pastured there for twenty-eight years, until I entered the monastery. That's when Rudolph moved out of my parents' home; he came with me to Saint Vincent. He is worn and torn, his antlers are tattered. Rudolph wouldn't sell at a flea market for 25¢, but then, I would never sell him. Rudolph is priceless, treasured, and so is the feeling that comes each year when I pull him out of the box and unwrap him. You see, in that first instant when I see him, I am a child again and all of the magic, all of the excitement of the Christmas season becomes almost tangible once more.

It seems to me a terrible shame that we allow ourselves to lose that excitement, that magic. Actually, we just give it away. We never grow out of it — we give it away. We toss it out every year in the rush to get cards out, to buy presents, to clean houses, to decorate, to get ready for parties. Hurry, hurry, rush, rush, rush!!! And for what???

In all the "busyness," we forget what we're really preparing for, and we lose that experience of magical anticipation which is not just for kids. Advent is supposed to be a time of joyful anticipation for adults, too. *Sing and rejoice, O daughter Zion! See, I am coming to dwell among you, says the LORD* (Zec 2:14).

This week, stop the rush! Take some quiet moments alone to unpack some of your favorite memories from Christmases past. Don't hesitate to revel in the childlike feelings they evoke and don't fail to recognize Christ's presence in your reminiscence. That's what really brings us the spark of joy; and, if a tear of sadness should happen to rise to your eye, let Him wipe it away for you, and always, always, always, give thanks.

# DOG DAYS

The dog days of summer — when we're in the thick of them, the lawns are browning, flowers are fading and spirits are languishing from the heat.

But just when we feel most like sitting around doing nothing, it seems that all of a sudden there's so much that needs to be done. Band camp and sports camps have begun in earnest and for those with school-aged children, the back-to-school preparation pressure is beginning to build.

For me too, the schedule is heats up. I feel the pressure mounting to prepare the lectures for the fall semester college classes. Yet in all of this, I feel the lazy, hazy days of the late summer luring me into a sleepy complacence. No time for complacency though. Work needs to be done! As it says in Scripture:

*a son who fills the granaries in summer is a credit;*

*a son who slumbers during harvest, a disgrace* (Prov 10:5).

Yet the ancient Jews always took the Sabbath rest. That's where we mess up — never taking time to relax. We just push and push and push ourselves.

In the midst of all your activity, try to find some special time to sit in your quiet space and rest. Enjoy the dog days, especially in the morning and evening when it isn't quite so hot. Too soon the days come when we find ourselves cooped up because of the cold and unable to enjoy the outdoors.

# ORA ET LABORA

I went to Carrolltown, where I served my deacon year, to rest for a few days before the fall semester at the college began. I was only able to stay there for a day and a half, but it was a wonderful time of rejuvenation for me.

One of the highlights of my brief stay in Carrolltown was my visit to Orchardvale Farm. It's a family-owned farm, operated by the Hoover family, whom I got to know while I was serving in Carrolltown. The farm has been worked by the Hoovers for four generations now.

After lunch, Chad Hoover gave me a tour. At the time, Chad was an eighth-grader and an altar server at Saint Benedict's. At Orchardvale Farm, two primary products are produced for market: potatoes and milk. Chad explained to me that his great grandfather had seen the wisdom of cultivating two non-related products, each of which could support the other in bad years.

Chad began by showing me the dairy operation. They have over two hundred cows there, all of them Guernseys. He showed me the calves, the milking parlor and how they calculate when each cow will deliver her calf. I was amazed to learn that calves are born during every month of the year. Chad showed me the equipment used to harvest the potatoes and even dug up some potatoes for me to see. He showed me the rows of pumpkins which he and his father cultivated for sale in the fall. Chad showed me how the corn grows, along with the oats for cattle feed.

Chad spent about two hours showing me how the farm operates. During this time, I sensed a young man keenly proud of his heritage and, at the same time, very humble.

At the end of each summer, when we celebrate the labor of workers, it seems fitting to stop and reflect on the creation story, which sheds light on the place of work and rest in God's plan. Trappist monk Charles Cummings, in his book, *Monastic Practices*, speaks eloquently on this topic when he writes:

*... the world was in a wild, uncultivated state until the LORD God created a human being 'to till the soil' (Gen 2:5). This human being (adam) was drawn from the ground (adamah), for it was 'out of the clay of the ground' that the LORD God formed this person and then 'he blew the breath of life into his nostrils' (Gen 2:7). 'The LORD God then took the man and settled him in the garden of Eden, to cultivate and care for it' (Gen 2:15). The first human being was not made to be idle, but to work in God's garden. The obligation to work was imposed on humanity in its original state, before the fall. Work belongs to the essential rhythm of a fully human life. It is natural for human beings to want to work, to enjoy working, and to experience the normal satisfaction of a job well done. (Cummings, p.49).*

Equally important as work, and also an integral part of our human identity, is the sacredness of and need for rest. We celebrate "Labor Day" by resting. Again from Cummings:

*The sabbath rest, of course, is an explicit precept in the Old Testament. 'The seventh day is the sabbath, the rest holy to the* LORD' *(Ex 31.15). So sacred was the sabbath command that work was punishable by death. Even beasts of burden were to rest on that day. If the sabbath rest was a duty, it was also a privilege. By keeping the sabbath, the creature imitated and participated in the repose of the Creator on the seventh day. 'God rested on the seventh day from all his work which he had done' (Gen 2:2). For human beings, to rest from work was a sign of a God-like freedom, dignity, and security. A slave was never permitted to rest from his work. The sabbath rest symbolized the liberation of the children of God and their sublime destiny of sharing the very life of God in his kingdom.* (p. 66).

When we celebrate Labor Day, rejoice in the gift of work in your life and the privilege of rest. It is one of the ways in which we show ourselves to be made in the image and likeness of God.

# SEEING THE SIGNS

*A man once had a friend who was a skilled potter. He often went to watch him at work as he molded the clay into various vessels. One day he asked his friend how he determined what he was going to make. The potter said he had discovered that when he was rested, he tended to make beautiful things, but when he was tired, he made more ordinary vessels for menial uses.*

*As the potter reflected on this, he concluded that when he was relaxed, he had both the ability to focus and the patience to make something beautiful. Oftentimes the process of making a perfect object involved crushing an almost complete vase or bowl back into a lump so that he might start over. Beautiful objects also required that he be much more careful at each stage. When he was tired, by contrast, he was less able to focus, less patient, and thus more apt to make mistakes and more likely to resort to making items that did not demand such precision.*

I think that this story makes a good point. Regardless of the type of work that any of us does, whether we're potters or painters, teachers or priests, it works in exactly the same way with us. When we are tired, we don't focus well; we don't have the patience we need to be as compassionate as our service demands.

When we recognize the signs that our ministry is diminishing, regardless of what form that ministry might take, the wise minister steps back, takes stock of his situation and takes measures to get back on track.

What are these measures? It seems to me that we could gain much by following the example of Jesus, whom the gospels tell us frequently went apart to a quiet place to pray. I imagine that Jesus did this when the demands of his ministry became too consuming. The press of the crowds, the challenges of the religious elite and the constant questions of his disciples would have made any of us weary. But rather than become snappish, Jesus would retreat into some brief moments of solitude to regroup. Maybe that's what we need to learn to do.

Consider your life. What are the warning signs that you are becoming stressed, tired or anxious? The best time to identify warning signals is when you are not feeling overtaxed. By the time you are feeling overwhelmed, it is impossible to see the situation clearly. Instead, at a calmer time, spend some moments thinking about the last time or two that things seemed to get out of hand. Think about how you felt physically and emotionally the last time you lost your temper. These are the warning signs to look for in the future. A certain level of fatigue, stress and anxiety is normal. But when it begins to exceed normal levels and spill over into other aspects of life, we need to be able to recognize the signs so that we can take prompt corrective action: retreat, rest and pray!

# DO IT NOW!

When summer comes, I find a lot of comfort working in my garden. It's supposed to be a meditation garden, so I attempt to create a certain mood. Trying to imbue a plot of land with a particular personality is more challenging than I thought. After every work session, when I sit back on my haunches, wipe the sweat from my brow and survey my efforts, I cannot help feeling like I need to do something more. Perhaps adding some perennials, or maybe planting something for a splash of color over in the corner might do the trick. Maybe if I just added some mulch right over there ...

Sometimes, what the garden really needs is simply for me to sit back, let everything grow, get a glass of iced tea, a favorite book and enjoy it.

Living is a lot like gardening. We make plans when we are young; a few like perennials, take root and flourish, while other plans wither away neglected for some other whim like annuals awaiting the first frost. Most of us spend our whole lives like fussy gardeners, adjusting this and trying that. We rush about playing politics and strategy in our work and in our personal lives as if our life will only have been worth living if we make it that way.

I'm too much of an existentialist to deny that our choices make our lives what they are, for good or for ill. However, if we spend all our time and energy trying to make things perfect for tomorrow, we miss today. And that would be regrettable. Why? Because life, the only one we're ever going to have, is today. If you want to find God, do not look back over your shoulder fretting about the past. God is no longer there. Do not anguish over the future, God is not present to you there either. Only in the *today* is God present to you. So open your eyes and ears to see His face and hear His voice in the people and events of this day. And do not waste it.

*He will renew your strength,*
  *and you shall be like a watered garden,*
  *like a spring whose water never fails* (Is 58:11).

Spend some time in your garden. Don't fuss in it, preparing it for some future time when you might take the time to enjoy it. Enjoy your garden now! The same can be said about your life, your husband or wife, your co-workers, your pets and especially your children. Life is happening to you and for you right now. Take the time to enjoy it — now.

# RETRO WISDOM

A few years ago, when I arrived at Christ the Divine Teacher School, where I made weekly visits to spend time with the students and teach religion, I found that they were celebrating a "retro" day. This meant that instead of their usual uniforms, the students were allowed to dress in the styles of the 1950s, '60s, and '70s. I scrapped the lesson I had planned, stepped back into the role of Social Studies teacher and presented a Sociology lesson. I asked the children about the clothes they were wearing and what they thought the clothing seemed to indicate about the personalities of the people who wore them back then. I talked about the political and social climate in those three decades and how it changed. My hope is that my students came away with more of an understanding of how the American culture evolved over the last half of the 20th century.

When I was driving back to the parish afterward, I found myself reflecting on the way in which our culture worked on me. I was a college student during the early '80s. It was the era of preppies, and we were socialized to work hard in school so that we would get good jobs and make a lot money. We became the yuppies of the second half of the '80s, obsessed with making money and climbing the corporate ladder — with gaining power and more and more possessions. The cultural impetus was so strong that it left me with a perfectionism and workaholism that can only be characterized as a personality defect. It led me to pursue an advanced degree in Business Administration. I certainly do not regret that decision, nor the skills I acquired. But when I entered the monastery, I found quite a contradiction to the values I had worked so hard to learn and espouse. I found that I had to learn an entirely new way of looking at life. The monastic way required me to slow down, to study the world around me, not out of profit motive, as though it were some new, untapped market to be developed. By the time I entered the monastery, that marketing approach already came naturally to me. Now I had to study the world for signs of the presence of God and His grace at work. The whole of the Benedictine monastic tradition is predicated on the natural ebb and flow of the rhythm of activity and rest in life, a rhythm that for the monk takes the form of a delicate daily balance between work and prayer. Striking this balance has not come easily for me.

Contrary to what some psychics and followers of "new age" philosophies say, we live only one life. So why give in to the rat race to do and gather more and more and more? We are not squirrels, with a frenetic compulsion to gather food against an uncertain winter. And just in case we feel so inclined, consider that more often than not, squirrels forget where they bury their treasures. Biologists tell us that their amnesia has been the source of more than a few forest groves.

As Christians, we are not called to be overachievers. Our purpose — the whole reason that God called each of us into existence — is to know, love and serve Him in this life and to be happy with Him forever in heaven. The book of Genesis tells us that as a consequence of Adam and Eve's foolishness, we must work:

*Cursed be the ground because of you!*
*In toil shall you eat its yield*
*all the days of your life* (Gen 3:17).

But God never intended that work should consume us. He confirmed the worth of leisure and rest at Sinai when He enjoined on the Israelites the Sabbath law. While the Sabbath rule insures a minimal level of rest for us, if we want to be truly happy, we need to balance work with prayer and leisure each and every day. Jesus Himself admonished His disciples, *"Come away by yourselves to a deserted place and rest a while"* (Mk 6:31).

Give some thought to your weekly schedule. Find places where you can create some space for holy leisure with those you love. They are God's gift to you. Don't forget to allocate some minutes for prayer each day, too. You'll find yourself happier, healthier and more energetic.

# WHAT'S YOUR HURRY?

Tom, the husband of a friend of mine, has worked at the same urban industrial complex for more than a decade. His drive to work usually takes between 45 minutes to an hour through a mostly barren landscape, partially along a river of a once-booming steel town. Tom is a great outdoors enthusiast and at one time used to plant a big garden.

As a youth, Tom spent a lot of time with his grandfather, who operated a nursery. His grandfather taught him a wonderful tradition, which he carries on to this day. Once a week, for one month every spring and every fall, Tom leaves 15 minutes early for work. He takes a small trowel and a few daffodil bulbs, and stops at a spot along his drive to work and places a few very carefully in the ground, where they are not likely to be disturbed. Then, for several weeks every spring he and the other motorists are greeted by the sight of bright yellow and white daffodils peeking out near trees, at intersections, and at places where the riverbank is not so steep that the daffodils cannot be seen.

Each spring, Tom gets weeks of pleasure from a few minutes work, once a week, for a few weeks each year. Each spring, he also makes it a point to drive along the country back roads where his grandfather did the very same thing. Each spring, he thinks a lot about his grandfather.

When my friend first told me about her husband's custom, I thought it was a very beautiful tradition. But then when I thought more about it, I came to realize that my friend's husband Tom is very wise. By spending a few minutes a week for a couple of weeks each year, he has improved the landscape that he and countless others must view on their way to work each day. His little planting custom has made his world more beautiful. But it has also made the world better for all those who pass that way when Tom's daffodils are in bloom each spring.

It seems to me that there are at least two lessons that we can learn when we consider the tradition that Tom's grandfather passed on to him. First, any of us can make the world a better place. We do not have to be destined for political greatness or civic heroism, though some might be called to just such greatness. But for most of us, the world can be made better by one small good deed at a time. Just as scenery along Tom's way to work has been made more pleasant one bulb at a time, so we make our environment better by each good choice we make. It requires just one choice at a time, one moment at a time, one day at a time. That is all it takes to make the world a better place.

The second lesson I gleaned from Tom's tradition has to do with patience. Tom's grandfather taught him to plant bulbs a few at time, not all at once. For the most part, whenever I start a project, I want to see results right away. I think that a lot of us are like that. But as I reflected on Tom's bulb planting, I was reminded that for some projects, we have to be willing to wait a long time. When we undertake a training program, a career path or even a fitness regimen, months and even years might be needed before we can see any clear result. Too often, I give up on the idea of starting a project because the result will not be big enough, or splashy enough, or prompt enough. Perhaps the wisest among us are those who undertake tasks like Tom's daffodils: tasks that make a subtle but lasting impact over time. After all Genesis reminds us that Lord God did not create the world in a day. Instead, he was patient and created little by little.

Whenever I feel the rush to "get a project over with," I pause to look out the window at the beauty God has created. I think about Tom's daffodils and the difference he has made through patiently persevering in his project over the span of a decade. Then I realize that life is not lived all in one day. Life is lived one day at a time. Then I say to myself, "What's your hurry?"

# BLESSINGS RENEWED

Spring is a wonderful season. I am especially grateful when we do not have a rush of hot weather as we do in some years, but a cooler, slower spring. Looking out the window the other day while I was eating lunch as I do each day with the Sisters at the Clelian Heights School for Exceptional Children, I was struck by the richness and variety of the shades of green all about. Then, yesterday, I found that the sisters had taken in a litter of baby rabbits which had been orphaned. I delighted in the time-liness of this rare find, since I have been teaching a unit on the Beatrix Potter literature with my classes, and had five real baby bunnies to share with them. After lunch today, we were treated to a visit from a local farmer who brought up two lambs for the children to see. Spring is a wonderful time of renewal.

I found myself thinking about the beauty of spring, and how God creates our world anew every year at springtime. I thought of how His presence is powerfully manifested in the rebirth that spring brings. I was reminded of a poem I had learned many years ago in English class, "Ode to Spring" by Anna Laetitia Bar-bauld (1743-1825):

*Sweet daughter of a rough and stormy sire,*
*Hoar Winter's blooming child; delightful Spring!*

*Whose unshorn locks with leaves*
*And swelling buds are crowned;*
*From the green islands of eternal youth,--*
*Crowned with fresh blooms and ever springing shade,--*
*Turn, hither turn thy step,*
*O thou, whose powerful voice*
*More sweet than softest touch of Doric reed,*
*Or Lydian flute, can soothe the madding winds,--*
*And through the stormy deep*
*Breathe thine own tender calm.*
*Thee, best beloved! the virgin train await*
*With songs and festal rites, and joy to rove*
*Thy blooming wilds among,*
*And vales and dewy lawns,*
*With untired feet; and cull thy earliest sweets*
*To weave fresh garlands for the glowing brow*
*Of him, the favoured youth*
*That prompts their whispered sigh.*
*Unlock thy copious stores.--those tender showers*
*That drop their sweetness on the infant buds;*
*And silent dews that swell*
*The milky ear's green stem,*
*And feed the flowering osier's early shoots;*
*And call those winds which through the whispering boughs*
*With warm and pleasant breath*
*Salute the blowing flowers.*
*Now let me sit beneath the whitening thorn,*
*And mark thy spreading tints steal o'er the dale;*
*And watch with patient eye*
*Thy fair unfolding charms....*

So often we find ourselves rushing through the day, whether to or from work, meetings, appointments or errands. In all this frenetic activity, I wonder sometimes if we fail to recognize the gift of God's handiwork all around us. If so, we miss out on so much. All of the beauty that surrounds us in springtime speaks of God's glory and His magnanimous generosity. In the beginning, He created this beautiful garden we call earth just for us. Each spring in His love for us, God recreates this garden. We can learn so much about Him just by taking a closer look at this gift. This spring, try to take some moments each day to enjoy the green all around us. It is God's gift to us, and a sign of His abiding grace. Regardless of the time of year or season of life in which we currently find ourselves, the promise of renewal is never far away. We need only to look around us to see this promise unfolding right before our eyes. But we need to be willing to rest, to take the time to notice, to relax into God's presence and be renewed. Consider how the birds and animals play. Perhaps they can teach us a lesson in accepting gifts gracefully and with humble gratitude.

# RELISHING ROOTS

I took a rare opportunity for a weekend off, loaded Bridget, Brendan and Braeca, my Gristmill kittens, in the car with some of their favorite toys, and we all went home for a weekend with Mom and Dad. In a tremendous stroke of luck, my sister Monica and brother-in-law Kevin were in from Ohio for the weekend with my three nieces and their golden retriever, Percy. My parents had quite a houseful, not to mention a regular menagerie.

It was a wonderful weekend, with much needed rest with my family and my pets. The kittens had a wonderful time — Percy did not. Bless his heart, Percy just wanted to be their friend, but the kittens didn't have the time of day for the poor dog. The presence of a great big pooch didn't slow them down for a moment. They romped all about my parents' large, screened-in porch, napped on the chaise lounge with their master and reveled in the attention they received from my nieces and the rest of my family. Just about everyone turned out to see this curious event when my mother, a dyed-in-the-wool cat hater, opened her home and her heart to not one, but three feline guests — and liked them.

One of the nicest parts of the weekend was attending Mass at my home parish as an ordinary member of the congregation.

As a parish priest, I rarely get the chance to hear another priest preach. Since we need to be preached to just as much as any other Christian, it was a delightful treat for me. I sat in the same pew we always sat in when I was growing up — the very last pew on the right. It truly was a homecoming for me.

As I sat there, enjoying the liturgy immensely, I found myself amazed. I had come full circle. Here I was, back in the church where I had been confirmed, attended Mass for more than two decades, where the CCD program had formed me, where I was nourished at the table of the Lord and where my vocation was nurtured and grew strong.

Consider your roots. How have your past experiences and relationships, good and bad alike, served to make you the remarkable person you are today? Give thanks to God for His hand working in your life and be patient — we are all works in progress. If everything in your life is not ordered perfectly to your liking right now, be patient, and recall that we are His project, not our own. As Saint Paul reminds us in his letter to the Christian community at Rome, *We know that all things work for good for those who love God, who are called according to his purpose. What then shall we say to this? If God is for us, who can be against us? He who did not spare his own Son but handed Him over for us all, how will he not also give us everything else along with him?* (Rom 8:28, 31-32). Perhaps we need to spend some time in prayer discerning His will for us. When our free choices conform to God's will for us, we find ourselves truly happy and at peace.

# THE SWEETEST MELODY OF ALL

There is a story that Jewish families tell to their children to help them understand the 3rd Commandment: *For six days you may work, but on the seventh day you shall rest (Ex 34: 21). As the story goes, one Thursday evening, the king asked his royal subjects, "What is the sweetest melody of all?" So early the next morning, Friday, the subjects gathered all sorts of musicians. The sound awoke the king, and all day long he listened to their tunes. But evening came and after listening to all of them, he still could not tell which was the sweetest sound. Finally one subject suggested they all play together, but it was so noisy, the king couldn't even think.*

*About that time, a woman, dressed in what we would call her "Sunday" best, made her way to the front of the crowd and stood before the king. "O king," she said, "I have the answer to your question." "Why didn't you come earlier?" he asked. She replied, "I had to wait until the setting of the sun." The musicians were still playing and the king told them all to stop.*

*The woman then took two candles and placed them on a small table before the king. She lit them just as the sun began to set. The flames glowed in the growing darkness. She then lifted her voice to sing. Her voice, like the candlelight, grew until it seemed to fill the*

259

whole room. "Blessed are you, O LORD, our God, King of the universe, who has sanctified us with the commandments, and has commanded us to kindle the Sabbath lights." She then said, "He who has ears to hear, let him hear."

Everyone was completely still. "What is that?" asked the king. He could not hear a sound. The woman then replied, "What you hear is the sound of rest, the sweetest melody of all."

This story probably never happened in real life. But the ritual the woman performed, the prayer she chanted, most certainly does happen — every Friday evening at sundown in devout Jewish homes. I was privileged, when I was just out of college, to be invited to the home of one of my Jewish friends on a Friday evening in August. My friend's mother performed the Sabbath ritual before the start of the meal. She chanted the candle-lighting blessing, in Hebrew of course, and I remember being awestruck by the feeling that this special time — this restful time — had truly been hallowed. Then I understood the commandment, and so this is a ritual that I perform myself when I want to dedicate a particular Sabbath in an extraordinary way to prayer, reflection and rest.

In Matthew's gospel, there is an account of Jesus' encounter with the Canaanite woman. As a non-Jew, she was a social outcast under the Jewish law of the time. Her daughter was afflicted with a demon and the woman begged Jesus for a cure for her. We can be confused because in Matthew's account Jesus seems to ignore her request initially — it seems harsh. Perhaps Jesus seems to ignore the woman only to accentuate the depth of her faith as she persists in begging Him for the cure. Finally, Jesus acknowledges the woman and cures the woman's daughter. Because of her faith, the woman finds rest from her worries about her daughter, and her daughter finds rest from her affliction. The Canaanite woman teaches us a powerful lesson about real faith and the holy rest that can be the fruit of such faith, particularly when we feel like an outcast.

When my twin nieces Lauren and Lyndley left to start college, it brought back many memories for me. Lauren attended my alma mater, the University of Pittsburgh. I remember how excited I was to start there in 1980. I thought for sure that I'd make new friends and that college life would be one grand adventure. I was wrong. In that first, seemingly endless, semester I spent at Pitt, I was utterly miserable. I had no friends, not even among my neighbors. I still don't know what I did or said wrong, but I was certainly an outcast. I had no friends — none. There I was, a scrawny kid from a small town, alone in a sea of humanity — how hard it was to find even one seat in the cafeteria where I wouldn't feel like I was intruding; an outsider on the fringe of someone else's group. An outcast.

As bad as life was for me at that time, as lonely as I was, that was when I learned to pray. This outcast learned to beg the Lord Jesus for help, for rest. That's why I can identify so readily with the Canaanite woman, and why I believe so strongly that faith and prayer can bring us rest in the worst of circumstances. And isn't that rest the sweetest melody of all? For me it sure was. That rest came in the form of one very graced young woman who befriended me and drew me into her wonderful circle of friends. Her generosity made all the difference. She was the instrument who brought me rest from my affliction. Because she chose to be kind to me, I had the most exciting four years of college that I could ever have wished for, full of great friends and good times.

Sometimes it takes years and a variety of seemingly separate experiences to piece together an understanding of certain events in our lives. This was certainly the case with my initial college experience. An autumn of affliction, discovering how to pray in my desperation, a kind voice outside the Biology building, the intimacy of a Jewish family's Sabbath meal — all piece together to make sense and wholeness grow from a broken heart. Prayer, faith, rest. Looking back, I wouldn't trade that first semester of college; not now that I understand what it was to teach me.

Sometimes we all feel like outcasts. But we aren't — not really. Jesus always welcomes us. Like the Canaanite woman, we need simply to persist in prayer and believe. Then we will find rest from our troubles — holy rest, peaceful rest, Christ's rest — a Sabbath for our weary hearts.